T H E
EXECUTIVE
STYLE
BOOK

Scott, Foresman Business Writing Series

T H E
EXECUTIVE
STYLE
BOOK

Patricia H. Westheimer with
Jacqueline S. Senteney

SCOTT, FORESMAN AND COMPANY
Glenview, Illinois   London

Library of Congress Cataloging-in-Publication Data

Westheimer, Patricia H.
    The executive style book / Patricia H. Westheimer, Jacqueline S.
Senteney.
        p.   cm.
    Includes index.
    1. Business writing.   2. Commercial correspondence.
I. Senteney, Jacqueline S.   II. Title.
HF5718.3.W47 1988
808'.066658—dc19   88–998
1 2 3 4 5 6 RRC 93 92 91 90 89 88   CIP

ISBN 0-673-38099-8

Copyright © 1988 Patricia H. Westheimer.
All Rights Reserved.
Printed in the United States of America.

Scott, Foresman Professional Publishing Group books are available for bulk sales
at quantity discounts. For information, please contact the Marketing Manager,
Professional Books, Professional Publishing Group, Scott, Foresman and Company,
1900 East Lake Avenue, Glenview, IL 60025.

ACKNOWLEDGMENTS

Many people gave us the support, advice, and encouragement that enabled us to finish this book with pleasure and pride. Specifically, we'd like to thank Chris Englert, Lee Ann Okada, Vicki Gibbs, and Tom Moffitt for their excellent research and critiques. Thanks also to Ken Senteney for his patience, support, and contributions. Special friends helped as well. We are especially grateful to Julius Westheimer, Gloria Westheimer, and Paul DuGré for staying with us when times were tough.

We also acknowledge the beauty, serenity, and comfort of La Jolla Cove.

PREFACE

What happens when you have to write a memo, letter, or report as part of your job? Do you put off the task for as long as possible? Do these typical excuses sound familiar?

- ○ I have to clean my desk.
- ○ I'll do it tomorrow; I'll have time.
- ○ I need more information before I can start.
- ○ I'll write it after I jog.
- ○ There's too much noise in this office.
- ○ Why can't I just call instead?

If these common excuses for putting off writing sound familiar, you're not alone. They are symptoms of writer's block, the most common reason that managers, executives, and, for that matter, all writers, give for not writing.

Writer's block is the inability to think of something to write. You have writer's block when you find yourself staring at a blank page or a blank computer screen and you can't think. It's as if all of a sudden you're brain dead. Nothing helps. You pick up your dictionary and find big words. Then you look at your reference books and find only the same old material. Nothing is new, nothing can help. With that motivation, and testimonial of experience, we wrote this book.

How is our book different from other business-writing books? First and foremost *we* — the authors — are different. We are former English teachers who have worked successfully with businesses to help them solve their communications problems. We now realize that what was once taught in our English classes is not relevant for today's business executives. In addition, much of what was taught was not up-to-date, and sometimes even inaccurate, for the correct business writer.

The good news is that your writing difficulties are not your fault! Formerly our students were taught that longer is better. It's not! In school you were taught to use fancy, complicated language to make you sound more powerful. That won't work. Finally, you were encouraged to write stories to entertain your readers, rather than to give them just facts. That won't work either.

So, let us re-educate you into the latest, most powerful, useful, and contemporary trends in American business writing. We have taught managers and executives how to achieve excellence in the competitive world of business by giving their ideas proper form and expression. Through our seminars, workshops, and private consulting, our SPEAKWRITE system has been especially effective in helping our clients overcome their fears and blocks about writing.

What we have discovered as a result of our combined experience is that there is a system to writing. Writing is a process; it benefits from a methodic approach. For our business clients, we have adapted this process approach to writing in a systematized format called SPEAKWRITE. It's a language that our clients understand, and you will too.

We hope you will employ the tools that this book provides. Use the book as a reference manual when you get stuck; turn to it for ideas on how to write your memos and letters. Feel free to "borrow" the examples and treat them like sample forms; plug in the words to fit your specific situation.

We begin our book with some rules and guidelines to correct writing. In the introduction, we explain why you must write well to stay where you are and advance up the corporate ladder. Your strong writing can make you an admirable example to your employees. In addition, with these specific guidelines you will be able to evaluate the writing of your employees and also screen job applicants for their writing-skills level.

In Part One we break down ways to create an individual executive writing style. The introduction, Chapter 1, tells you when to write instead of when to use the phone. In Chapter 2 we discuss style, along with ways to create excitement and flair in your sentences and paragraphs. We also show you how to avoid jargon, cliches, and passives. In Chapter 3 we talk about good grammar and ways to master it. Specifically, we discuss major problems in grammar, including lack of agreement, inconsistent tenses, non-parallel phrases, and weak transitions. We offer suggestions and examples for correcting these basic, common flaws. Chapter 4 details specific guidelines for correct punctuation. Then, in Chapter 5, we tackle spelling and give you quick tricks for improving your techniques to master correct spelling of misspelled words. Finally, Chapter 6 discusses modern standards for the use of nonsexist language.

In Part Two we get down to the "business" of writing. In Chapter 7 we introduce you to SPEAKWRITE and its five simple steps, and then in Chapter 8 and Chapter 9 we apply these specific SPEAKWRITE guidelines to memos and letters. We show you several poor writing samples of these specific types of documents, followed by examples of how to improve these samples with the SPEAKWRITE System. Here you can insert your own executive style.

Part Three is concerned with word processors and writing, and tools of the trade. In Chapter 10 we discuss the word processing revolution. How does it relate to your writing? We direct this part of our book toward those who are already using word processors; it is not an introduction to word processing. In this chapter we also discuss the advantages and pitfalls of electronic mail. We describe how to turn the word processor into a time-saving friend. In the last chapter, Chapter 11, we list valuable resources so that you can stock your own or your company's library.

In the Appendix, we provide several handy lists. Keep them in a convenient place, and they'll become close and valuable friends.

It is our hope in writing this book to take the pain out of writing and to help you tap into the most valuable writing resource—you. When you adopt and practice the techniques presented in this book, we know you will become an efficient and powerful writer. As a result, the writing process will become less painful and more enjoyable to you.

CONTENTS

PART TWO

PUTTING IT ALL TOGETHER

7

Mastering the SPEAKWRITE System 71

8

Writing Winning Memos 107

9

Producing Powerful Letters 127

PART THREE

HELPING YOURSELF TO THE TOOLS OF THE TRADE

10

Word Processors: Allies or Enemies? 165

11

Resources 181

Appendix 191

Index 219

PART ONE

CREATING INDIVIDUAL STYLE

CHAPTER 1

Introduction

Many executives feel that it's easier and faster to pick up the phone and call rather than to write. Or better yet, it's even easier to let their secretaries do the work for them. But both solutions leave powerful people feeling less competent and less independent. The written word is powerful because it makes its point in permanent form. People forget many things—times, dates, and meetings. Although they may still forget something when it's written down, they can't then blame you for not providing them with the information. The written response is also a reference. There can be no mistake in understanding the information—unless it is poorly written. When there's doubt about who said what, a written document provides proof.

There are many reasons to write, and many types of documents convey these reasons. There are letters asking for money (commonly referred to as collection letters), proposals, contracts, procedures, manuals, applications, employee evaluations, and rejection letters. In addition, some of these types of documents have to be filed for legal purposes, for archival purposes, or for reference. When you write these different kinds of documents, make sure they are clear. Signals can get crossed because of poor writing.

Ann, an executive for a soft drink company, had problems with her new computer. Loading programs and other start-up procedures were difficult, so she wrote a letter to the computer company asking for an updated manual. However, she created a communication problem because she wrote her letter when she was angry and frustrated; the letter came across as a complaint rather than a request. The company therefore sent her information on how to return her computer for a full refund, rather than a manual explaining what she needed to know.

In any document that you write, the purpose should be evident and the message clear. We have provided some example situations and example documents to address the situations.

Suppose you've been interviewing candidates for an assistant management position for your division. You've narrowed your candidates to five finalists, and you've finally made your choice. How do you inform people that they're not qualified for jobs while still keeping open a possibility that they might work for you in the future? How do you inform the person you want to hire? If you're like most employers, you'll call your new hire with the good news and write the others the bad news. We suggest that you go one step further and write them all. Write the new hire a nice, friendly letter, something like this:

Dear Allison:

Welcome to our team! We really enjoyed our interview, and we've decided that we want you to work for us. Your qualifications and strong personality will mix perfectly with our department.

Congratulations, Allison. We look forward to seeing you on your first day and working with you thereafter.

Sincerely,

Nathalie Burg
ABC Corporation

NB:dc

You might write the less-qualified candidates a polite letter such as this:

> Dear Phil:
>
> We enjoyed your interview. Unfortunately, we can't offer you a position with our company right now. Please feel free to resubmit your resume if you are interested in applying for other job openings at ABC Corporation.
>
> Thank you for taking time to interview with ABC Corporation. Good luck in your job search.
>
> Sincerely,
>
>
> Nathalie Burg
> NB:dc

Remember, your new candidate may not take the job; or if she does, she may not work out. Allow the other candidates to feel that you considered them carefully for the job, and encourage them to reapply for other positions. You probably don't want to telephone them with the bad news; it is an uncomfortable situation, and they may start asking questions you have no desire to answer. Take the time and make the effort to write an upbeat, friendly letter. Doing so may serve you well later. To ignore these job-seekers and not respond at all is both an act of rudeness and poor business procedure. Many people don't write necessary letters and memos simply because they are insecure about their writing skills. They don't want to look "dumb," so they don't write at all. Necessary communications don't get transmitted; valuable information gets lost. How sad!

Perhaps one of your employees just secured a big sales contract. You could call her up and congratulate her. Or, if you happen to spot her in the coffee room, thank her. However, who else will know about it? And how can she keep your verbal thanks in her files? The more effective and powerful approach is to write her a memo of recommendation with copies to your boss and your boss's boss. You will have a proud employee, and you'll look good, too. After all, you hired her, didn't you? Of course she's good!

Here's a sample of a memo you might send her:

> To: Patricia
> From: Wanna
> Date: August 2, 1987
> Subject: FANTASTIC EMPLOYEE
>
> Hear ye! Hear ye! Another outstanding employee has captured a huge sales contract!
>
> Congratulations, Patricia, for catching San Diego Construction. I know you've been working on them for a long time, and ten points go to you for your persistence. Once again, good job, Patricia!
>
> cc: T. Allen
>   J. Garafolo

What do you do when there is a policy change within your organization? Do you call a meeting and announce it? Or do you write a memo detailing it? If there's no discussion on the subject, you can save time by writing a memo. If it's a standard uncontroversial change, a memo will be more efficient than a meeting, and it will document the news.

> To accommodate both smokers and nonsmokers, the following hours will be in effect immediately for the Terminal Room:
>
>   Nonsmoking—Mornings until 12:00 Noon
>   Smoking—Afternoons from 12:00
>
> There will be no smoking in the nonsecure terminal room, or the TRV room.
>
> JPF:krb

However, if there is a controversial policy change, like an increase of hours with no increase in salary, a memo won't work well at all. We know of one company that did just that. They increased hours without increasing salary. To make matters worse, they also installed time clocks and said they were for security. Finally, they announced the news company-wide via a cold, impersonal memo from the Chairman of the Board. How would you respond to a memo such as this:

> Effective immediately, working hours will be extended one hour to 6 p.m. I expect excellent output in this last hour of the day.
>
> Thank you.
>
>
> Mr. Fuentes, COB

Employees felt disgruntled, and morale fell to an all-time low. If you're required to announce something negative such as this, put it on a more personal level. Obviously you need to formalize such a change in writing. Although you still won't be favorite manager of the year, the following type of memo might help:

> We just received a huge contract from San Diego Construction. Because of the increased workload, I'm extending work hours by one hour. The work day will now be 9–6 p.m. I know this may cause some hardships, but in the long run the extra output will decrease our work. Plus, at year's end there may be a bonus for everyone.

Have you ever had to call up one of your favored clients and ask her to pay her overdue bill? What was the effect? Perhaps if the phone call was the last resort before turning the case over to your attorney, the call was probably an effective tool. However, a phone call without a letter is probably of little or no effect. Following is an example of a friendly but firm letter requesting payment. It reminds your client of the nonpayment and assumes that he must have "overlooked" the invoice.

> Dear Ron:
>
> Enclosed you'll find another invoice for work done a few months ago. We realize that you've been busy, but please pay this invoice promptly.
>
> Thank you.
>
>
> Diane Cloke
> ABC Corporation
>
> Encl.
> DC:cl

Remember, if you value this client, you must be careful if you want to continue doing business, while at the same time protecting your reputation and your company's interest. Once the letter is written and sent, it's there forever. So make sure the notice is congenial, especially if you send it to a personal acquaintance.

All the previous examples attempt to prove that in certain business situations, the written word is a more powerful tool than is the spoken word. Of course, as a busy executive, you probably spend a great deal of time on the telephone. Perhaps some of that time should be spent writing. On the other hand, some points of business are best handled by a brief phone call. You, of course, must make the choice. We will help you decide when to choose the written word over the spoken word. We will teach you how to write from a position of confidence and to refine what you have already written. We will emphasize that more is not necessarily better and that longer is not necessarily clearer. So let's get started.

In our next chapter, we will discuss creating your own executive style.

CHAPTER 2

Achieving Writing Excellence

COLOR AND EXCITEMENT IN
YOUR WRITING

TACKLING TONE

JARGON AND GOBBLEDYGOOK

ACTIVE VOICE AND PASSIVE VOICE

STRONG VERBS

CORRECTNESS, CONCISENESS,
AND CLARITY

COLOR AND EXCITEMENT IN YOUR WRITING

A five-page memo from another department just landed on your desk. You see by the title that it concerns a matter that directly affects your unit. The pertinent facts are presented in a seemingly logical order. Yet, you discover that the memo could substitute for your bedtime glass of warm milk. Smooth, yet bland, the writing lulls you into a trancelike state. The result? You're forced to return again and again to the opening paragraph and reread the entire memo because you slept through the significant points.

In its structure, there is nothing wrong with the writing. It's just that when the writer composed it he neglected to add two important ingredients—color and excitement. Oddly, these two items are almost always conspicuously absent from most business writing. It seems there's some unwritten rule passed from generation to generation of businesspeople which states: "Thou shall not create business communications that can in any way be construed as interesting or exciting."

Today, many people recognize this concept as misguided. They want to make their writing more colorful and readable, but they don't know how. All types of writing, especially business and government writing, use jargon-filled, stuffy, pompous language. In other words, the writers remove themselves from their writing. The first step toward curing the lack of appeal in documents is to put yourself back in your writing.

Writing style is very personal. That doesn't mean that you must aim for Pulitzer Prizes or strive to fill even the shortest of letters with purple prose. It means that you should relax a little and let some of "you" come through. Ask yourself, "How would I say this if I were sitting across the desk from this person instead of writing to him?"

You wouldn't consider walking into a colleague's office and saying:

> Per our conversation on the phone . . .

Yet millions of letters which begin just that way are received daily in offices throughout the country. Why not write it just as you would say it:

> Here's the background information we discussed
> on the phone yesterday.

In creating your own style, beware of using techniques that make you sound the way you think you "should" sound rather than the way you do sound. Relying on that type of artificiality is what gave business writing a bad name in the first place.

The only technique that will help you effectively develop your own style is a good, clear understanding of the language and its rules. Strunk and White, in *The Elements of Style*, point out that

> "A careful and honest writer does not need to
> worry about style. As he becomes proficient in the
> use of the language, his style will emerge, because
> he himself will emerge . . ."

Following are some hints to help encourage that self-emergence and lead you to a clear and simple writing style full of color and excitement:

○ Write about people, not abstractions:

Instead of	Try
Department Head	Sally Wellington
They	Bob, Robin, and Shayna
You	We, us

○ Talk to your reader, using personal pronouns (I, you, he, she, we, they).

Instead of:

A review meeting is held every three weeks.

Try:

We hold a review meeting every three weeks.

Instead of:

It will be necessary to talk to the chef.

Try:

You'll need to talk to the chef.

○ Put more of yourself into your business letters by including the recipient's name somewhere in the body of the letter. Look how friendly an ending using this technique sounds:

Let me know your thoughts on this, Vicki, so we can start soon.

TACKLING TONE

One last note about putting yourself into your writing. Even if you have yet to create a style of your own, there is a certain amount of your personality apparent in your writing, and that is your attitude toward your audience.

This is known as your "tone." Try as you might to obscure it with long words or with friendly sentences, your readers will always recognize when you patronize them. It's essential to adopt a tone of respect; this is a precept that is stated by many authors of books on writing. Always keep this thought in mind whether you're writing a short memo or a long proposal.

Instead of patronizing your reader in this way:

> Although I realize such an important person might be busy, could you fit it into your busy schedule to attend the annual meeting?

Try using this tone of respect:

> I know you're busy, but I'd appreciate it if you would plan to attend our annual board meeting.

Writers who patronize often manipulate and border on false flattery and sarcasm to get what they want. Respectful writers use honest, direct, and nonmanipulative language to achieve their goal.

JARGON AND GOBBLEDYGOOK

A sure sign of sloppy, lazy writing is the overuse of clichés. Clichés substitute an overly used statement for an original thought. Also, they can mean different things to different people. When you use a trite expression, you risk not having your meaning understood. Rather than reaching for some tired expression that's been used by everyone, use your own words. Describe what you mean!

Instead of:

> What's the bottom line?

Try:

> How much will we spend on this investment?

Not only will you avoid boring your reader, you'll also make your message easier to understand. It's crisp and fresh, too.

Here are some familiar business clichés you can permanently banish from your writing, along with some replacements:

INSTEAD OF	TRY
What's the bottom line?	What is the result?
Let's touch base soon.	Let's meet soon.
Don't reinvent the wheel.	Try not to complicate the matter.
Let's take the line of least resistance.	Let's do the least controversial thing.
Let's keep our options open.	Let's be flexible.
Can we drop back and punt?	I'm not sure about this; what do you think?
We've been playing telephone tag.	We've been trying to speak for a while.
It's a real can of worms.	This subject is complicated.
Let's clear the air.	Let's discuss any problems.
Can we get to the bottom of this?	Let's conclude this discussion.
It looks like they want to play hardball.	They're being difficult.

Another way to relay your message clearly is to avoid jargon and gobbledygook. Consider this jargon-filled sentence written to an executive secretary:

> Initialization is required prior to installation and must be carried out globally.

That mess may mean something to a computer programmer, but to the rest of us it sounds as if something of great magnitude is about to happen worldwide—but we're not sure exactly what it is.

Jargon can be an efficient shortcut in explaining specialized concepts, but only if your audience understands it. Otherwise, using jargon obscures your message and frustrates your reader. Some people use the jargon or language of their own profession (legalese, businessese, educationese) in addressing people outside their spheres, thinking that it will impress them. Usually the opposite is true. The purpose of language is to express, not to impress. Use language that does not call attention to itself in order to make your writing clear, natural, and easily understood by everyone who reads it.

Jargon has a close relative you'll also want to avoid—gobbledygook. This term, credited to the late Congressman Maury Maverick, refers to speech or writing that is difficult to understand because of overuse of involved sentences, technical terms, and "big words." It seems to be a favorite style with business and government.

To avoid being trapped by jargon, try to keep your sentences under twenty words; choose short, concrete words instead of long, abstract ones; and use jargon only when you're sure your audience is familiar with the terms.

ACTIVE VOICE AND PASSIVE VOICE

An important way to strengthen your writing is to move from the passive voice to the active voice. This is a subtle but effective shift. When trying to understand the difference between the passive and active voices, think in terms of the types of people you know. A passive person lets things happen. An active person makes things happen. The same is true in business writing. Passive voice verbs delay the action; they let the action happen to the actor. Active verbs take charge and do the action. They form a smoother sentence. Here's an example of a sentence with the passive voice:

The desk was cleared by the custodian.

Who's supposed to be the actor in that sentence? The custodian. Yet, that person is receiving the action. All you have to do to move your sentence from the passive to the active voice is to ask yourself, "Who is doing what to whom?" In that sentence the custodian is doing the action to the desk, so switch the word order around.

The custodian cleared the desk.

That change does three very important things. First, it shifts the sentence from passive to active; you have the doer accomplish rather than receive the action. Second, you eliminate the weak *be* verb and substitute an active, strong verb, *cleared*. Third, you tighten and shorten your sentence.

You win when you move from the passive to the active. A verb in the passive voice combines any form of the verb *to be* with the past participle of the main verb; that is, the passive uses *am, is, are, was, be, being, been*, plus a main verb that usually ends in *en* or *ed*. In this sentence:

> Adequate protection will be required by each
> department.

Who are the actors? Just shift them to the beginning of the sentence. It now reads:

> Each department will require adequate protection.

If you want the sentence to be more direct, put the verb in the present tense:

> Each department requires adequate protection.

It's tighter, cleaner, and more direct and effective.
   Here's another example:

> She was considered incompetent by her manager.

That sentence uses the passive voice. It's more powerful this way:

> Her manager considered her incompetent.

Use of the active versus the passive voice also brings up the issue of responsibility. Many people hide behind the passive and duck responsibility for something they feel, decide, or do. Many performance evaluations use passive voice verbs, especially when they deliver bad news. They may say:

> The management report was not finished by
> Nathan.

Instead of the more direct:

> Nathan did not finish the management report.

The following letter needs a dose of active voice:

> Dear Mrs. Smith:
>
> The manuscript entitled "The High Cost of Running a
> One-Man Show" which you sent to my attention has
> been received.

> Approximately every four to five weeks a review
> meeting is held. After the review meeting you
> will receive notification of the decision of the
> review board.
>
> Thank you for your interest.

That message would be much stronger and clearer, had the writer presented it this way:

> Dear Mrs. Smith:
>
> I received your manuscript, "The High Cost of
> Running a One-Man Show."
>
> We will hold our next review meeting in four or five
> weeks. We will discuss your idea at that time. I will
> notify you of our decision then.
>
> Thank you for your interest.

A good way to know if you write in the passive voice is if you use the word "by" and follow it with what should be the subject of your sentence. For example:

> The memo was issued by the marketing manager.

Instead write:

> The marketing manager issued the memo.

In a passive sentence the verb always comes before the word *by*, and the person who should be the subject follows.

STRONG VERBS

In addition to using the active voice, the best way to add power to your writing is to use action verbs. The central word in your sentence is the verb. It's the only part of speech that can really accomplish action for you. Most people rely on weak or inactive verbs rather than strong and powerful ones to drive their sentences. Consequently, their sentences sit rather than move on the page. That's exactly the opposite of what you want to accomplish. It's not always possible to avoid weak verbs, but stay away from *to do, to make, to seem, to appear, to be,* and *to get.* All are grammatically correct, but they lack power.

Let your verbs work. Look at this sentence:

> A decision was made by management to charge
> each unit that makes use of the equipment.

The weak verbs show up again: *was* and *make.* Without searching for new words at all, you can tighten that sentence by writing this:

> The management decided to charge each unit that
> uses the equipment.

These simple changes create power and impact for the entire sentence.

Certain nouns tend to smother active verbs. *Authorization* is one of them which is particularly popular in the business world.

> Authorization for the purchase was given by the
> vice president.

How about writing:

> The vice-president authorized the purchase.

You may notice that words ending in "ion," such as *authorization, production, hesitation,* and *completion* also smother verbs. It's easy to turn these nouns into verbs that will create more powerful business writing. We include more action verbs in the Appendix.

Verbs can be your greatest allies in business writing. Search for them and treasure the strong ones.

CORRECTNESS, CONCISENESS, AND CLARITY

Education as a whole has its Three R's—reading, 'riting, and 'rithmetic; and strong writing has its Three C's—correctness, conciseness, and clarity.

BE CORRECT

The previous section on grammar insures that your writing will be correct. Verbs should agree with their subjects, and pronouns with their antecedents. Your thoughts are parallel, and your tenses are concise. Your mastery of transitions makes your writing flow. There is a list of frequently misspelled words in the Appendix. Keep it handy. We have provided the list to help make your writing correct.

BE CONCISE

Closely related to correctness is conciseness. You have a much better chance of keeping your reader's attention if you keep your communication brief and to the point. There are many ways to improve on conciseness. Here are a few tips:

- Use short sentences—preferably under twenty words.
- Always opt for shorter words.
- Keep paragraphs short and to the point. We mentioned earlier that there is no standard length, but a guideline of four to eight sentences is helpful.
- Eliminate unnecessary words.

Here's an example of a paragraph that we can significantly shorten with just a little pruning:

> My partner, Marie Edmonds, and I are very
> excited that you have agreed to work on a consult-
> ing basis as our editor for this book proposal.
> Please give us your overall comments about our
> approach as well as specific editing remarks on
> the letters and survey questions. We would also
> appreciate your suggestions with regard to the
> selection of a working title. I've included a list of
> candidates we've been considering.

Watch what a little judicious cutting can do:

> My partner Marie Edmonds and I are excited
> about working with you. Please comment on our
> approach to the project, and edit the letters and
> survey questions. We also need a working title and
> would welcome your input. See the attached list of
> possibilities.

By tightening the language and removing the unne-cessary words, we shortened this paragraph by four complete lines.

○ *Do Away with Redundancies:* Saying something one time, clearly, should be enough. If the reader didn't get your point the first time, she can always go back and reread it. Here are some common redundancies that often show up in business writing:

> advance *forward*
> basic *fundamentals*
> circle *around*
> *close* proximity
> combine *together*
> consensus *of opinion*
> cooperate *together*
> continue *to go on*

factual truth
important essential
refer *back*
repeat *again*
visible *to the eye*
enclosed *herewith*

A close relative of redundancy is wordiness. Redundancies make your writing wordy, but a writer can also be wordy without being redundant. For clarity it is often good to repeat key words within a paragraph. But it can be overdone, as in this wordy paragraph:

> A board of directors meeting is held approximately every four to five weeks. After the board meeting you will receive notification of the decision of the board.

Eliminating the three uses of the word *board*, and putting the paragraph in the active voice shorten it considerably.

> We hold a board of directors meeting every four to five weeks. After the meeting we will notify you of our decision.

○ *Edit Out Prepositional Phrases:* They weigh down your sentences. Instead use simple prepositions. To do this, take a second look at any phrases that start and end with a preposition. See if you can say the same thing with just one preposition. Here are some examples:

Instead of	Try
along the lines *of*	like
in order *to*	to
in regard *to*	about, for
in the area *of*	in
in the event *of*	if
on the part *of*	by
with reference *to*	about

○ *Use the Active Rather Than the Passive Voice:*
Doing this can cut your word volume by as
much as one-third.

BE CLEAR

The final "C"—clarity—represents the essence of writing.
The whole idea behind any writing, and business writing
in particular, is to get your message across. Whether you're
promoting a new product or justifying a raise, you want to
be understood.

Everything covered in this book helps you get your message across as clearly as possible. In addition to the grammar, spelling, and punctuation guidelines, here are some
other brief tips to keep in mind when striving for clarity:

○ *Be Concrete and Specific:* The more specific
you can be, the less likely you are to be
misunderstood. If you just request a magazine on economics in Africa, you may end up
with *National Geographic* when what you really
wanted was *Time*. In their television commercials, a beer company has made humorous
and effective use of the need for being
specific. When a patron steps up and orders a

"light," the patron receives a flaming arrow or a light bulb. This is far from the light beer that was really wanted.

○ *Use the Right Words:* If you mean *infer* (to draw a conclusion by reasoning), don't write *imply* (to indicate without saying outright).

> Every gesture she made *implied* her impatience.

> I *inferred* from his comments that I had confused him.

To help you choose the right word, keep both a dictionary and a thesaurus handy. But be cautious of excess usage of synonyms. We will talk more about this later.

○ *Put Main Ideas Up Front:* Doing this makes it easier for the reader to get your point. Many fine American authors make a practice of placing the subject and verb of each sentence at or near the beginning of the sentence and almost always together. You should follow this practice.

○ *Include One Idea Per Sentence:* Pompous, flowery writing usually gets you into trouble because it tries to include too many ideas in one sentence.

○ *Use Lists:* In business especially, lists can prove invaluable for getting your ideas across clearly and succinctly.

○ *Use Headings, Sometimes Called Headers:* Like lists, headings can make your writing easier to understand. They break up the expanses of the written word and clue the reader to what's coming. Both margin and paragraph headers will improve your readability.

○ *Make Items Parallel:* The section on parallelism in Chapter 3 strives to make everything you write parallel. That applies to parts of speech as well as ideas and concepts.

○ *As a Final Test for Clarity, Give Your Writing the "Who, What, When, Where, Why" Test:* See if you accomplish what you set out to do. Who is responsible for doing whatever is required? What is supposed to be done? Have you explained the "when," "where," and "why"? If you are satisfied that you answered each of these questions in the clearest manner possible, then you probably accomplished your purpose for writing. Your reader will respect and appreciate the clear and informative document, and recognize you as an accomplished writer.

CHAPTER 3

Translating Grammar into Good Writing

Good grammar is essential when you want your business writing to be accurate and effective. Even though formalities are changing, there's no excuse for ignoring traditional and important principles of effective grammar and style. Those are the ideas that we discuss in this chapter.

We're going to outline the most important stylistic requirements that will make your writing not only conversational and easy to read, but also correct in respect to the proper guidelines of grammar, punctuation, and style. Those are the skills that separate a powerful, polished writer from a sloppy, hasty one. You might think, "What's the difference? If I write the way I speak and say what's on my mind, what does it matter if I have a sentence fragment or a run-on?"

It makes a big difference! It's like choosing to appear at work in a messy, mismatched suit versus one that is carefully put together. An attitude of precision will send promotions and acknowledgments your way.

It's true that your memos, no matter how parallel and consistent, may never hit the bestseller list. But you do want them to make it to the top of your supervisor's desk. A polished writer knows what makes a successful impression. Consistency and agreement are the backbone of this success.

GRAMMAR VERSUS STYLE

It's important to understand the difference between style and grammar. Style is the flair, the way you put your words together, the techniques you use for creating flow. It's how you choose words that stand out on the page to remain memorable, exciting, and powerful. Grammar provides the building blocks to help you accomplish that style. Effective, correct grammar makes your style even more powerful. With lack of agreement, tenses that don't match, pronouns that don't agree, and sentences and paragraphs that are poorly combined, your writing won't work. First, let's examine these building blocks. Then we'll decide how to put them together to create a style that is truly your own.

Returning to school for a grammar course or a business English class just to learn all the parts of speech, diagrams, and ways to put the words together isn't necessary. There are certain basic grammatical principles you can master right here; that's all you need to know. These principles will not only help you in your own writing but will also give you a sharp eye for evaluating the writing of the people who work under you and those who work alongside you.

In the following pages, we've listed the grammar terms alphabetically. Use them like a dictionary of grammar, and refer to them when you are unsure whether the sentences you're writing are strong and grammatically correct.

AGREEMENT

The important principle here is that a verb must agree with its subject in both number and person. A singular subject always takes a singular verb. Likewise, a plural subject must have a plural verb.

> *Singular:* The new copy machine works well.
> (machine works)
>
> *Plural:* The new copy machines work well.
> (machines work)

Remember, adding an *s* or *es* to a noun makes the noun plural; adding an *s* or *es* to a verb makes the verb third-person singular.

NOUN + S

The software programs run well.

The phones ring loudly.

VERB + S

The software program runs well.

The phone rings loudly.

Don't let other nouns and pronouns in a sentence confuse you. The subject is the important noun and the only one to agree with the verb.

> The carton of books and papers is heavy.
> (carton is)

Generally, the number of a verb is not affected by inserting between the subject and the verb any expressions beginning with such words as *along with, as well as, including, in addition to, not to mention, accompanied by, together with, with.*

> *Cost,* as well as delivery date, *influences* the bid.

Identifying the correct verb for a compound subject can sometimes be confusing. Keeping in mind the following rules makes this task easier.

1. Subjects joined by *and* are usually plural.

    > *The president and his managers want* to see this.
    >
    > *Alerting the staff and notifying the board take* hours.

    o   Use a singular verb when two or more subjects joined by *and* refer to the same person or thing.

    > The *founder* and *president lives* in Denver.

    (The verb refers to the same person.)

    o   Use a singular verb when two or more subjects joined by *and* are preceded by *every*, *each*, *many a*, or *many an*.

    > *Every* blouse, dress, and skirt *has* its own tag.

2. Subjects joined by *or* or similar connecting words usually take a singular verb when they are singular and a plural verb when they are plural.

    > *Robin or Elizabeth answers* the phone during meetings.
    >
    > *Meetings and memos* are helpful.

3. If one of your subjects is singular and the other plural, the verb usually agrees with the nearer subject.

    > *Neither* the colors nor the *appearance has* changed.
    >
    > *Neither* the appearance nor the *colors have* changed.

4. Watch out for inverted word order (verb + subject) or the structure *there* + verb + subject. Don't make a mistake because of the inverted order.

VERB + SUBJECT:

Into the crowded boardroom *came* the newest *employee.*

THERE + VERB + SUBJECT:

There *were papers* and *folders* on the desk.

5. When used as subjects, indefinite pronouns such as *each, either, neither, one, everybody,* and *anyone* take singular verbs.

> *Everybody* in the organization *needs* training.
>
> *Neither takes* cream in his coffee.

6. Look at the context to determine whether subjects such as *all, any, half, most, none,* and *some* need a singular or a plural verb.

> *Is* there *any* of the coffee left?
>
> *Are* there *any* of the books here?

7. Some indefinite pronouns, such as *both, few, many, others,* and *several,* are always plural.

> *Both were* interviewed.
>
> *Few are* bold enough to ask questions.

8. Some words which appear to be plural are actually singular, and when they are used as subjects, they take singular verbs.

> electronics
>
> physics
>
> measles
>
> economics
>
> summons
>
> lens
>
> news
>
> mumps

> The *news* from the home office *is* depressing.

CONSISTENCY OF TENSE

A commonly made and easily corrected mistake is a shift in tense.

> *Incorrect:* I *left* the office and *try* to catch a cab.
> (shift in tense from past to present)

> *Correct:* I *left* the office and *tried* to catch a cab.

You probably know whether or not you have used the correct tense by the way something sounds when you take the time to read it. But in our rush to get letters and other documents finished and distributed, we often fail to revise what we've written and overlook mistakes of this type. A simple way to correct these inconsistencies in verb tense is to be certain that all the verbs are in the same tense.

How would you fix this sentence?

> When she noticed the door being pushed open she yells for help.

The best solution is:

> When she noticed the door being pushed open, she
> yelled for help.

A good way to check for inconsistencies in your verb tenses,
as well as to find if your overall piece is strong, is to read
your writing out loud. You'll be surprised at how mistakes
surface when you read your work aloud.

Here's a final note on tenses. The present tense is
the most immediate, powerful, and easy to use. Try to
include it whenever you can. Your reader stays with your
topic, relates to your message in the present, and takes
action—now!

PARALLELISM

Expressing parallel ideas in similar form increases the
clarity and impact of your writing. This concept is called
"parallelism," and it's simple to use. Just remember, nouns
should be paralleled by nouns, infinitives by infinitives,
adjectives by adjectives, subordinate clauses by subordinate clauses, and so on. Read the following examples and
see how this rule of creating parallel construction works.

> *Nonparallel:* The new brochure was *colorful* and
> *written very well.*
>
> *Parallel:* The new brochure was *colorful* and
> *well-written.*

"Colorful" is an adjective, but "written very well" is the
verb and its modifiers. Thus, the words are grammatically
nonparallel. In the parallel version "colorful" and "well-
written" are both adjectives and therefore balance the
sentence.

Nonparallel: This personal computer is *light-weight, easy to use,* and *it doesn't cost much.*

Parallel: This personal computer is *lightweight, easy to use,* and *inexpensive.*

In the nonparallel version, the first two modifiers are adjectives, but the end of the sentence is an entirely new clause, not a single modifier. The sentence is, therefore, unbalanced. In the revision, the three adjectives are balanced and parallel. They create a sentence that's easy to read.

Parallelism is especially important when writing items in a list. This list has all the pieces, but because they're not expressed in parallel form, the list is difficult to follow.

Nonparallel: The duties of the new board president are:

- o To oversee meetings
- o Attend official functions
- o Managing the office.

Parallel: The duties of the new board president are to:

- o Oversee meetings
- o Attend official functions
- o Manage the office.

or

Parallel: The duties of the new board president include:

- o Overseeing meetings
- o Attending official functions
- o Managing the office.

When you use parallelism, remember to deliver what you promise. If you use correlative conjunctions like *both . . . and, either . . . or, neither . . . nor, not only . . . but also, whether . . . or,* they should be followed by elements in parallel form.

Nonparallel: Either we meet the deadline or lose the account.

Parallel: Either we meet the deadline or we lose the account.

Nonparallel: We sent letters both to the *New York Times* and *The Wall Street Journal.*

Parallel: We sent letters to both the *New York Times* and *The Wall Street Journal.*

PRONOUNS AND ANTECEDENTS

Another mistake that signals sloppy writing is failure to make sure that pronouns agree with their antecedents (the words for which the pronouns stand) in number, gender, and person. A singular antecedent (one that takes a singular verb) requires a singular pronoun. Likewise a plural antecedent needs a plural pronoun.

Singular: The top *salesman* never loses *his* perspective.

Plural: The *managers* try constantly to update *their* staffs.

Always use a singular pronoun when the antecedent is a singular indefinite pronoun, such as:

anyone	everyone	someone	no one
anybody	everybody	somebody	nobody
anything	everything	something	nothing
each	every	either	neither
each one	many	one	another

One large organization had *its* own gym.

Every office has *its* own computer.

Use a plural pronoun when the antecedent is a plural indefinite pronoun, such as *many, few, several, others, both*.

> *Several* clients felt *they* had been neglected.

Some indefinite pronouns may be singular or plural, depending on the noun they refer to. They are *all, none, any, more, most*.

> *Most* of the chapter is written, but *it* doesn't include everything.

Most refers to *chapter* and is the antecedent to *it*.

An antecedent consisting of two or more nouns joined by *and* requires a plural pronoun.

> *Tom and Mary* said *they* can't make it.

> *IBM and Xerox* are way ahead of *their* competitors.

Two or more singular antecedents joined by *or* or *nor* require a singular pronoun. If one of the antecedents is singular and the other plural, the pronoun usually agrees with the nearer antecedent.

> Will Tom *or* Bill need *his* ticket?

> *Neither the staff nor* the managers met *their* goals.

Trying to make the genders of certain pronouns agree with their antecedents can create a problem if you want to avoid sexism in language. (We will discuss how to avoid sexism in your writing in detail later.) Instead of the traditional method of using the masculine pronoun to include both sexes or either sex, many modern writers choose to use plural pronouns to refer to singular antecedents that denote both sexes or either sex.

Instead of:

An *employee* needs to feel *he or she* is valued.

Try:

Employees need to feel *they* are valued.

or

Employees need to feel valued.

SENTENCES AND PARAGRAPHS

Trying to write anything—except maybe a poem—without using sentences and paragraphs is like trying to build a house without a hammer and nails. Sentences and paragraphs are the basic building blocks for communicating in writing. They are so basic that once you've learned about them, you tend to take them for granted. That can be dangerous!

As you probably learned back in elementary school, a sentence is a group of words expressing a complete thought and containing a subject and a verb (predicate) along with any complements or modifiers.

Most of us know how to recognize a run-on sentence (The production meeting was useful, everyone went away with specific assignments.) and a sentence fragment (Because the sales team had yet to get organized.). Beyond that, however, we rarely stop to think about the importance of sentence structure. Varying sentence length and structure is a simple way to add interest to everything you write. Compare the following paragraphs.

> The operations department will be moving to the second floor. We will make the move on Friday, October 2. We will not be accepting business calls on the afternoon of October 2. If you have pressing business on that day, please contact administrative assistant Joan Miller at extension 3002.

Notice that every sentence in the previous paragraph begins with the subject and follows a similar pattern. The writing sounds choppy and boring. See if the rewrite, using the same information, sounds better.

> Friday, October 2, is our moving day. The operations department will transfer to the second floor. During that afternoon we will not accept business calls. If you have pressing business on that day, please contact administrative assistant Joan Miller at extension 3002.

Here are some rules to follow when striving for clear yet interesting sentences.

Vary sentence structures by using the following:

○ *Simple Sentences:* I left the office.

○ *Compound Sentences:* I left the office, but had to return for the mail.

○ *Complex Sentences:* If I don't put the mail by the *door*, I always forget it.

○ *Compound-Complex Sentences:* I want to get a mail holder to put by the office door because I keep forgetting to take the mail when I leave. That might be a costly mistake one day.

Vary sentence beginnings by starting with the following:

○ *The Subject:* Gossip always starts at the coffee machine.

○ *A Prepositional Phrase:* In the office at the end of the hall is a perfect location for the copier.

○ *An Adverb:* Quickly she restacked the reports.

The key to adding interest to your writing without sacrificing clarity is to balance short sentences with longer ones.

But try to keep the long ones to twenty words or less. If they're much longer, they can become bulky and confusing.

When you put together several related sentences which develop one unit of thought, you've got a paragraph. By breaking ideas up into individually organized, simple-to-understand chunks of thought, you make it easier for the reader to understand your content.

There is no rigid rule for standard paragraph length. While writers suggest not making a paragraph more than eight to ten lines long, there will be instances when that's not enough space to complete the thought. Likewise, you don't want to make your paragraphs too short. The best approach is to think about developing your idea completely, rather than worrying about the length of the paragraph.

The look of your letter is also important. You need enough breaks between paragraphs to create "white space" or "air" on your page. A general though not rigid rule is to open with your main idea, use an example, illustration, or fact to support it, and then wrap the thought up. Five or six sentences should accomplish this well; sometimes you'll use even fewer.

Here's an example of a topic sentence developed further throughout the paragraph.

> *Money spent to install hazardous waste management systems in plating and surface finishing shops can also have economic benefits.* An increasing number of owners and managers are realizing that by preventing pollution, changing processes, upgrading facilities, detoxifying wastes and recycling, they reduce operating costs and become more competitive and profitable. They also avoid potential liability claims.

TRANSITIONS

As your reader moves from paragraph to paragraph of your letter or document, your organization must be clear, and the writing should flow. You can accomplish this by using effective openings, clear topic sentences, and smooth transitions.

Transitions are words and phrases that help your reader move easily from one idea to the next. Such expressions as *also, besides, in addition, briefly, as a rule,* and *by contrast* make your writing easier to follow. We've included a list of transitions in the Appendix. Use them between paragraphs and sometimes even between sentences. Sprinkle them sparingly throughout your writing. One per paragraph is generally enough.

Another way to move smoothly between paragraphs is to take a word from the last sentence of one paragraph and use it in the first sentence of the next paragraph. Here's an example:

> . . . Why then did The Pacific Century Group make the decision to headquarter here?
>
> According to Muckerman, the favorable economy and comfortable climate had to do with the decision.

Single sentences can also function as a transition between paragraphs. For example:

> The latest trend today suggests using reader-based writing. This means that you write for your reader rather than for yourself. It is a critical orientation to remember at the beginning of any writing project.
>
> *Contrary to the notion of reader-based writing, most memos begin with and are consumed with the pronoun "I."* Now, how important is "I" to the reader? Not very. Successful salespeople know to target their product or their service to their

customer. This is the key to get them to buy and use the product. It's the same with effective writers. So, instead of using "I," "me," "us," or "we," why not focus instead on "you," "your," client's name, or client's concern?

To help you make this shift, here's a quick tip. If it's too difficult to write in your audience's voice, do your first draft on your own. Then when you revise your memo, change your orientation from writer-centered to reader-centered.

Headers, to announce the contents of the following paragraph, can also be an effective way to make a transition. Look at this example of a header:

Showing Your Key Ideas: Finally, have you highlighted key ideas and indicated their relationships? You can do this by underlining, listing, and phrasing them in parallel form.

Headers also announce key topics, provide visual variety on the page, and let your reader find important information quickly and easily. Use them for both one-page and longer memos. They're contemporary and increasingly popular with business writers and readers. All of these techniques add class and clarity to your writing. They show you as a sophisticated, controlled, and careful writer.

CHAPTER 4

Punctuating
Like a Pro

Punctuation is vital to strong writing. In fact, the best writers know that inaccurate punctuation can ruin clever ideas and creative phrases.

Punctuation is so large a subject it actually demands an entire book. In fact, we present it in eight-hour sessions for our clients . . . And that barely covers commas! That's why we strongly recommend that in conjunction with a good grammar and reference text, you purchase a punctuation manual. We list several in the reference section of this book.

Just like clothing fashions, styles of punctuation change. The current trend, which journalists call "down style" is to use fewer rather than more marks of punctuation on the page. Whatever this year's fashion, always use enough punctuation to make your writing clear. Certain sentences are more understandable with just one comma instead of four.

Following are some facts about punctuation that every good business writer should know.

CONTROLLING COMMAS

Commas can be killers. They are the most frequently used punctuation mark and can therefore cause the most problems. English has dozens of rules for using them, and your grammar reference book will list them for you. But the important thing to remember about commas and business writing is this: their main use is to help you correctly and clearly communicate your meaning.

If left unchecked, comma confusion can cause some serious communication blunders as the writer of the following sentence learned:

> The student trainees, who are described in this
> evaluation, did not meet our criteria.

Reading that, the personnel office was ready to halt the entire student training program. What the writer meant was that some of the students–those described in the evaluation–were not working out. The rest were probably doing a fine job. What he should have written was this:

> The student trainees who are described in this
> evaluation did not meet our criteria.

What a difference a couple of commas can make! By enclosing the clause "who are described" with commas, you tell the reader that the clause could be removed and the sentence would mean the same thing. By removing the commas, the reader perceives that the sentence must be read all together to get the correct meaning.

An even stronger way to write this sentence to avoid confusion would be:

> The student trainees described in this evaluation
> did not meet our criteria.

So be sure to use commas to set off a subordinate clause only if the main clause can stand alone, unchanged, without it.

Another spot where writers often misuse commas is between two or more adjectives. Many people automatically think that if there is more than one adjective, there must be a comma. Not so. The rule is this: Use commas to separate two or more adjectives only if the noun could stand alone, unchanged, without any of them. Take this sentence:

She is a knowledgeable, talented instructor.

This could be broken into two sentences: She is knowledgeable and talented. She is an instructor.

She is a knowledgeable economics instructor.

If we try to separate this we get this: She is an instructor. She is knowledgeable and economics. It doesn't work. To get the true meaning we need to know that she is an economics instructor.

An easy easy way to tell whether your sentence needs a comma between the adjectives is to remove the adjectives altogether and put them in a sentence alone (She is. . . .). If when you do this, the noun means something different and the adjectives make no sense alone, then you need no commas in your sentence.

Another problem area is created when commas are used instead of periods. Editors call this a "comma splice," or a run-on sentence. For example:

She ought to have heard the phone, I let it ring ten times.

The punctuation mark here should be a period, not a comma. Commas should create a brief pause within complete sentences. The period's task, on the other hand, is to separate independent clauses. A comma and conjunction or a semicolon can also separate independent clauses.

Some of the other places that require commas are between items in a series, between lengthy introductory phrases and clauses, and between two clauses separated by conjunctions. Just remember that the comma is a powerful and an effective mark of punctuation for separating thoughts and phrases in your business writing.

When they begin to write, many people develop "comma fever." When they don't know what else to do with their punctuation, they insert a comma just to show any kind of pause or break. Although the comma is a necessary punctuation mark, its use can be overdone. You don't want to break up the flow of a sentence unnecessarily. In fact, keep in mind a Westroots rule: if you don't have a reason to use a comma, leave it out. If you use too many commas, your sentence will sound choppy rather than connected. Readers are more offended by excess punctuation than not enough.

Avoid sentences like this:

> Tom, please read, edit, and repage this report,
> then, print out a new, edited version, so that
> Lillian, the account supervisor, can have a clean
> copy.

Delete commas and any other excesses. If you need to, begin new sentences where commas exist. For example:

> Tom, please read, edit, and repage this report.
> Then print out a clean, edited version for Lillian.

MASTERING SEMICOLONS AND COLONS

Knowing how to use semicolons and colons correctly can be confusing. Most people run into problems because they don't really know what these two punctuation marks are for, and they incorrectly try to substitute one for the other. Look at the sentence below and see how the writer has correctly used the semicolon:

> The outline was created by our systems division;
> the final proposal was completed by our network-
> ing unit.

That's one long sentence that could have been divided into two or separated by a comma and a conjunction. But the two parts of the sentences are closely connected, and the semicolon shows the close link between them. Also note that after the semicolon, you do not use a capital letter. The unit is technically one complete thought. An alternative revision could read:

> The outline was created by our systems division,
> but the final proposal was done by our net-
> working unit.

Both examples are grammatically correct. It is up to you to choose the style you want. By using either one, you can add variety to your business writing. Remember, use a semicolon as an alternative to a period to indicate a close relationship between two independent clauses.

Close cousin to the semicolon is the colon. The most effective use of the colon in business writing is to introduce a list. The colon means "the following" and should never be used following a verb or preposition. So when you write a sentence with a list of items to follow, the colon works this way:

> The VISA Credit Card can also double as an ATM
> Card and perform these services:
>
> ○ Get cash from Checking Account, Savings Account,
>   VISA Account, and CreditLine.
> ○ Transfer funds between accounts.
> ○ Make loan payments.

You can also use a colon in a sentence containing a list. A polished marketing consultant wrote about his plans.

> Next year we'll develop three new supermarkets:
> Buyright; The Superstore; and Best Buys, Inc.

Note that he placed semicolons between the items in his list. That's because one or more of the items in the list (Best Buys, Inc.) already contains a comma. When that happens, use semicolons to separate your items.

PARENTHESES PROFICIENCY

Many people use parentheses when they don't know exactly where to place an idea. They reason, "Well, if my reader doesn't want to read this, the reader doesn't have to, but I'll put this in parentheses just to cover myself." That reasoning won't work, especially in business writing. It breaks the flow of an otherwise smoothly written memo or letter. It also distracts the reader from your main point or idea. Look at the following excerpt and see how the writer puts a major body of information in parentheses.

> The HHS must designate at least ten surgical procedures for which a second opinion will be required. Cataract surgery (since optometrists are defined as physicians by Section 1861 of the Medicare Act, it can be assumed that HCFA will permit them to offer the second opinion!) is sure to be listed.

The response of most readers is either confusion or disgust. People don't want to fight through copy in order to understand it.

If you are not sure certain material is important enough to be in your document, don't enclose it in parentheses. Leave it out entirely. If it is important, do not put it in parentheses. Putting it in parentheses relegates it to a status of lesser significance, and the reader will ignore its importance.

When you must use information in parentheses, the best way is to enclose your entire sentence. The worst way is by beginning a sentence, putting a parenthetical unit in the middle, and then completing your sentence, as was done in the example above. It doesn't work well stylistically or organizationally. You can improve the sentence by re-writing it this way:

> The HHS must designate at least ten surgical procedures for which the second opinion will be required. Cataract surgery is surely to be listed. (Since optometrists are defined as physicians by Section 1861 of the Medicare Act, it can be as-sumed that HCFA will permit them to offer a second opinion!)

The other place where parentheses are necessary is when you include a lengthy name of a company or document and then tell the abbreviated form or acronym. The pa-rentheses will hold the abbreviation or acronym form so that you can continue to refer to that throughout the rest of the memo or letter. This is an acceptable and necessary way of indicating an abbreviation or acronym. However, don't use abbreviations in your memo unless you are certain your reader knows their meaning.

> For almost ten years, Small Business Association (SBA) has offered an innovative, federal financing guarantee to help ease economic pain for small- and medium-sized businesses.

APPLYING ACRONYMS AND ABBREVIATIONS

While on the subject, let's say a few words about acronyms and abbreviations. While they can be great time and space savers, use them sparingly. A good rule is to spell out all words and phrases which would be puzzling if abbreviated. When you do abbreviate, do so correctly. Since several thousand abbreviations exist in the English language—with new ones added every day—it is always good to check a dictionary or other reference for the correct spelling. Some examples of acronyms are these:

North Atlantic Treaty Organization (NATO)

Screen Actors Guild (SAG)

Strategic Arms Limitation Talks (SALT)

Program Evaluation and Review Technique (PERT)

School to Employment Program (STEP)

Employee Assistance Program (EAP)

If you think even a few of your readers might not understand an acronym or abbreviation, spell it out the first time you use it. If you explain it early in a document and then don't refer to it again for several pages, spell it out again. Don't frustrate your reader.

Some writers use acronyms to "one up" their readers. They include acronyms generic to their own company. They are the only ones who understand these acronyms. By using this "in" language, they try to intimidate or overpower their readers. The ploy, however, usually backfires. The reader feels estranged from the material, the issue, and the writer. Go easy on acronyms; they can intimidate rather than ingratiate your reader.

USING QUOTATION MARKS

Quotation marks are necessary and functional marks of punctuation. Most people know that quotation marks are effective in indicating what someone has said. The problem is not when, but how, to use them. Below are the basic uses for quotation marks:

1. Periods and commas always go inside quotation marks.

   "This is where our staff wants to live," he reports.

2. Semicolons and colons always go outside quotation marks.

   Yesterday he said, "I'm leaving for Chicago tomorrow"; however, he's still here today.

3. Exclamation points and question marks go inside or outside the quotation marks depending on the sense of the sentence.

   Did you see "This Week on Wall Street"?

   She asked, "Are you going to the conference?"

   She yelled, "Stop it!"

   She said, "I wonder who the new manager will be?"

Again, a complete grammar reference book will also give you sound guidelines for using quotation marks correctly, but those three rules should help.

Punctuation need not be a terribly complex subject, and you certainly don't have to go back to seventh grade English in order to learn it. However, understanding correct punctuation and using it consistently will increase your confidence and strengthen your writing.

CHAPTER 5

Defeating Spelling Demons

SPELLING AIDS

QUICK TRICKS

It seems as though certain people are blessed with a knack for correct spelling; others have trouble getting their name down right. Most of us probably fall somewhere in between.

To insure that your business writing is always free of spelling errors, buy a few good reference books and use them religiously. Also, be aware of your own personal list of spelling demons—those words you can never seem to get right—and concentrate on learning how to spell them correctly.

One successful attorney admits to being a weak speller. "But I've learned to overcome part of it," he says. "I dog-ear my dictionary for the words I repeatedly have to look up. That way I don't waste time searching for the same words over and over. I go directly to them."

Borrowing from this technique, why not create your own list of words you constantly misspell. That way you can quickly consult your list, find the word you want, and copy its spelling.

The benefit of the second technique is that the more you look at the exact word you want, the quicker you'll learn to spell it on your own. Other research shows that most people have two alternative spellings for words that give them difficulty. Try writing out both ways; your eye will generally take you to the correct one.

Finally, a successful lecturer says, "I present many, many seminars where I write on a chalkboard. I carry a spelling list for reference."

SPELLING AIDS

The best way to avoid misspelling is to use some high-quality reference books. Even if you consider yourself an adequate speller, no amount of experience or knowledge of rules can take the place of a good dictionary. Some books that we find helpful with spelling rules and lists of misspelled words are:

The Gregg Reference Manual, Sixth Edition, by William A. Sabin, McGraw-Hill, 1985.

Harbrace College Handbook, by John C. Hodges and Mary E. Whitten, Harcourt Brace Jovanovich, 1986.

The Brief English Handbook, by Edward A. Dornan and Charles W. Dawe, Little, Brown and Company, 1984.

Webster's New World Misspeller's Dictionary, Simon & Schuster, New York, 1983.

QUICK TRICKS

Use your spelling reference. If you want to save yourself the time and energy of always having to refer to these books, try to master the principles of spelling. The books listed above clearly lay out the most common spelling rules (*Gregg* in particular). Study these rules until you have a good grasp of them. This will take some work, but it will pay off in the long run not only by saving you time, but also by making your writing stronger and more effective.

To improve your spelling further, make a list of those words for which you find yourself frequently consulting the dictionary. Then use some of the following techniques to help you master their correct spelling:

○ Visualize the correct spelling of the word. Write it down and notice how it looks on the page. Then look away and visualize it. Do this until you can see the word, correctly spelled, as it looks on the page.

○ Write the word down several times to help you break an old habit and replace the habit with a new one.

○ Carefully pronounce the syllables of each of your spelling demons. If you use the correct pronunciation of difficult words, you can start correcting some of your misspellings.

○ Proofread your work for misspellings. One of the best ways to do this is to start at the end of your document and read backwards. By doing that, you can see every word separately and, the content of the piece doesn't distract you.

If you do your writing on a word processor and have access to a spelling checker, by all means use it. These programs are not perfect; they won't question the use of incorrect but properly spelled words (for example, *advice* instead of *advise*). They are, however, a real timesaver for checking typos and other incorrect spellings. Look at the list of commonly misspelled words in the Appendix.

Suggestions on the Use of Gender

Our writing reflects our attitudes. We communicate our sexism, biases, prejudices, likes, and dislikes about issues on which we are not even writing. In this chapter, we focus on attitudes that apply to business writing and provide you with Westroots techniques that work.

PRONOUNS

WHAT TO DO WITH *HE*

No one has come up with an English pronoun that includes both sexes when the sex of the person is unknown. In school we were told to use *he* when the sex of the individual was unknown. Our teachers told us *he* was generic and neutral. They taught us to say this:

> When seeking an attorney, always check his credentials.

or

> When seeking an attorney, always check his or her credentials.

For the plural, we said this:

> When seeking attorneys, always check their
> credentials.

All of these sentences are grammatically correct. But the first sentence is the weakest. *His* is no longer neutral although we learned that it was. By adding *his or her*, you include all persons without offending anyone.

IS *ONE* USABLE?

Academic writing accepts the use of the pronoun *one*, but business writing doesn't. The following sentence sounds too stuffy and just doesn't work:

> One must pay one's bills on time.

A possible solution is to eliminate the pronoun altogether, and use a noun as in the following example:

> People must pay their bills on time.

works better than

> He or she pays his or her bills on time.

The worst is this:

> S/he pays his or her bills on time.

You don't speak this way. Besides, how do you pronounce *s/he*?

So, what do you do? Here are some suggestions.

○ Use the plural forms of pronouns when
  possible and avoid all references or use of the
  generic *he*, *his*, or *him* when referring to a
  "typical" individual. Although in the past we
  considered this "neutral" terminology, it
  excludes females. Avoid referring to the sex

of a person except when mentioning a specific individual.

Instead of:

> The Credit Manager wants his invoice paid upon receipt.

or

> The Credit Manager wants his or her invoice paid upon receipt.

Try:

> Credit Managers want their invoices paid upon receipt.

or

> David Watson, the Credit Manager, wants his invoice paid upon receipt.

○ If you're writing a lengthy document or report, it's often easier to put your nouns and pronouns in plural form to avoid a gender choice.

Instead of:

> The Customer is always right. Company policy has long supported this credo. When dealing with a customer, listen to his side of the story first. . . .
>
> After you've heard his version of the complaint, ask the customer how you can satisfy him.

Try:

> Customers are always right. Company policy has long supported this credo. When dealing with customers, listen to their side of the story first. . . .
>
> After you've heard their version of the complaint, ask them how you can satisfy them.

○ Eliminate pronouns when appropriate or when your subject focuses on an individual that may be of either sex.

Instead of:

> When dealing with a customer, listen to his side of the story first. . . .

Try:

> When dealing with customers, listen to both sides of the story.

Here is another example.

Instead of:

> The compliance officer may enter the premises when he/she presents proper identification.

Try:

> The compliance officer may enter the premises after presenting proper identification.

○ Occasionally use the pronouns he or she to avoid stereotyping sex into certain occupations. Doctors and lawyers historically have been men; teachers and secretaries historically have been women. When the sex is not specified, follow these examples.

Instead of:

> The doctor saved the life of *his* young patient.
> The secretary works well with *her* boss.
> The lawyer defended *his* client in a tough case.
> The teacher works hard on *her* lesson plans.

Try:

> The doctor saved the life of *her* young patient.
> The assistant works well with *his* boss.
> The lawyer defended *her* client in a tough case.
> The teacher works hard on *his* lesson plans.

MAN

Man is no longer a generic term. In 1788, the world had a different attitude. *Man* included everyone. In 1988, however, the fact is that *man* is not all inclusive. It excludes *woman*. In general, avoid the use of man.

Here are some further guidelines.

INSTEAD OF	TRY
manhood	adulthood
man or woman	people, person, anyone, or some-one
chairman or chairwoman	chair, official, or executive
policeman or policewoman	police officer
fireman	firefighter
salesman or saleswoman	salesperson, sales assistant, sales representative
spokesman	spokesperson
Englishman, Irishman, Frenchman	English, Irish, French, etc.

Instead of:

The man who comes late will be docked in half-hour increments.

Try:

Latecomers will be docked in half-hour increments.

JOB TITLES

Certain occupations have traditionally excluded males or females, and thus stereotypes have emerged. Times have changed and the boundaries have been lifted. Our language is changing: new words enter our vocabularies daily. Fifty years ago the chairman ran the conference. Today the chairperson does.

New job or professional titles replace the previously held gender-specified positions. Here are some examples:

INSTEAD OF	TRY
steward, stewardess	flight attendant
usherette	usher
poetess	poet
maid, cleaning lady	cleaning service
office boy, office girl	office worker
tailor, seamstress	alterations specialist
watchman	guard
handyman	helper
newsman, anchorman	reporter, newscaster
craftsman	artist
mankind	humanity
mailman	mail carrier

From this list, you can see it's not always just a matter of changing nouns like *man* or *woman* into *people* or *person*.

Sometimes you may even have to rewrite your sentences, as in this example:

Instead of:

> After the contract is signed, our manpower needs will triple.

Try:

> After the contract is signed, our personnel needs will triple.

MS., MRS., OR MISS?

What is the female equivalent of *Mr.*? *Mr.* doesn't identify the male's marital status, whereas *Mrs.* and *Miss* do so for females. The problem with the female address is when to use which.

In the business world of the 1980s, it is appropriate to address women, regardless of marital status, with *Ms.* before their name. Traditionally, *Mrs.* signifies married women, and *Miss* identifies unmarried women. *Ms.* is the female equivalent of *Mr.*

However, some women find the *Ms.* title offensive, especially if they feel *Mrs.* is more respectable. Ideally, finding out their preference is the best strategy.

An alternative is to drop the title.

Instead of:

> Deborah McCarthy was the keynote speaker for the National Zoological Society banquet. Ms. McCarthy spoke about fund raising activities. . . .

Try:

> Deborah McCarthy was the keynote speaker for the National Zoological Society banquet. She spoke about fund raising activities. . . .

```
To:        Everyone
From:      Margarite
Date:      August 15, 1987
Subject:   FILING CHANGE
```

We will be changing our filing policy starting September. The county recorder now requires that all escrow papers have our company logo. Although this may be a hassle at first, convenience will replace the preliminary inefficiency.

If you have any questions about the policy, I'm always around to lend a hand.

Thanks!

MC:tl

Attitude. All the previous factors affect audience attitudes. How does your audience feel about you and your subject matter? Are they positive, negative, or neutral? Keep their attitudes in mind; ignoring them gets you into serious trouble. Nothing discourages a worker more than receiving a memo written with no one in mind. He's not sure what he's supposed to do, if anything. He may wind up throwing it in the trash! Even worse, your audience may feel neglected, discounted, or plain insulted. Win them over with a personalized, individualized approach!

Here's a memo written on a "touchy" organizational change. The writer, a division manager, knows the people in his division are already blatantly opposed to the change since it means some staff cutbacks. Notice how he considers their attitudes, yet lets them know the change will still occur. But he does it with their concerns in mind. After all, he wants his group behind, not opposing, him.

We will reorganize our word processing pool starting July 10. Our goal is to increase efficiency while still maintaining a pleasant working environment. We will set new goals for everyone, and of course we'll compensate you all in the end. We've got a busy year

coming up. I know with good attitudes from all
players we'll come out winning.

Finally, in considering your audience, ask yourself
these questions:

○ Who will read this?

○ What position(s) do they hold?

○ How well are they acquainted with the
subject matter?

○ What special interests or personal preferences
do they have?

○ What do I want from them? Action? Approval? Appreciation?

○ How do they feel about my topic?

○ How are they likely to react to it?

TONE

Tone reflects your style of speaking, the inflections, the
mood, and the level of formality or informality you use in
communicating. The tone you employ with your staff
might not work as well with the company president. Tone
is just as important in writing as it is in speaking. Have you
ever said to anyone in a conversation, "I don't like your
tone of voice?" What were you referring to? Chances are
you were talking about the anger or hostility in the speaker's voice. Perhaps, in another situation, you felt that a
person's tone conveyed appreciation of you or of your
actions. You can tell what a person is thinking or feeling
from the tone of voice. Your writing translates this principle. Remember, what you write is your personal advertisement. You're selling yourself, your company, and your ideas.

Tone is not necessarily mood. Mood refers to how you feel at a given moment: angry, sad, happy, excited, or depressed. Yet you can be in a rotten mood and still write a cheerful, friendly memo to your employees. It's easier to write upbeat memos and letters if you're in a good mood. If you're angry or depressed, be careful not to let your negative mood appear in your writing.

Notice these two examples. The first is written by the Executive Vice-President and General Manager of a contracting firm. He is concerned that employees adhere to Working Paper guidelines. This excerpt from his memo reflects his worry and concern. It is overly formal and authoritarian.

> The definition of a Working Paper is an accumulation of notes, drafts, drawings, etc. to assist in the formulation and preparation of a finished document, and these can be either classified or unclassified in nature.
>
> Certain requirements have been established by the Defense Investigative Service in regards to the marking and logging into the accountability system of Working Papers. At the commencement of writing a Working Paper, the first requirement is the date of creation being affixed to the first page, or title page (if any). The next requirement, if the document is to be classified, is the conspicuous marking of all pages, top and bottom, with the overall classification of the document. These markings may either be stamped or printed, but should be of larger size than the writing or printing of the document. Classification markings indicated for paragraphs, portions, subjects, and titles (if known) should be entered as the document is being created.

The second example is written by the same manager, a month later, after we helped him revise it. The second memo, which is more upbeat, reflects the positive attitude and sincerity of the writer.

A Working Paper (WP) accumulates notes, drafts, drawings, and other documentation. WP's can be classified or unclassified. Either way, the Defense Investigative Service sets requirements for marking and logging WP's.

○ Put the date on the title page or the first page.

○ If the WP is classified, mark all pages with a classification sticker.

○ Enter all classification marks as you produce the document.

Thank you.

PURPOSE

It's important to have your purpose in mind before you begin to write. Are you writing to inform, respond, refute, inquire, direct, or persuade? Once you know your purpose, the organization and focus of your correspondence become easier to determine.

A trouble area for many executives and managers is writing too much at one time. Avoid this. Keep a clear direction and focus on one topic at a time. If you're writing a memo, it should have only one major purpose. The same is true for a short letter. For a long letter, proposal, or report, there may be several purposes. If so, separate the different subjects with headers or subject titles. The important point is to organize the purposes clearly and discuss them one at a time.

RESULTS

"Results" refers to what you want as a result of your writing. You might ask yourself, "Do I want an appointment, a raise, a contract, a telephone call, or a promotion?"

If you can't come up with a result, maybe you don't need to write at all! Perhaps a quick phone call will do the job. However, if you do need to write, and you do want something as a result, it's critical that you keep your outcome in mind before you begin to write.

Again, the four critical elements of SPEAK IT:

○ Audience

○ Tone

○ Purpose

○ Results.

PLAN IT

By now you're probably thinking that you're ready to start writing—you've done all your preliminary work, researched your audience, determined your purpose, written out what you want. Isn't it time to sketch a quick outline and start writing? Not quite. Let's talk about prewriting and freewriting.

PREWRITING

The most important stage of your writing is the "Prewriting Stage." We suggest you try using some, or all if necessary, of the prewriting techniques when you get stuck or experience "writer's block." Prewriting involves techniques to help you develop thoughts, break through writer's block, and organize your ideas. These prewriting techniques are quite different from the traditional outlining techniques you were taught in school. Outlining is a left-brain function, the logical, analytical side of your brain. Outlining helps to organize your ideas. That's not a bad approach, unless you don't have any ideas. Where are these ideas supposed to come from? Here's where prewriting techniques prevail.

Prewriting taps into your right brain (the more creative side) and helps you develop thoughts that are already there. Ideas emerge in a random, free-flowing fashion. You now have a greater range of ideas and creativity than the traditional outlining approach permits.

Prewriting consists of three basic techniques:

○ Brainstorming

○ Mindmapping or clustering

○ Organizing.

It's important to remember that you don't have to use all these techniques every time you write. They are tools to help you unblock your mind, tap into your ideas, and get them down on paper. In some cases, you may need to use all of them. In others, maybe you'll use only one or two.

In writing this book, we approached each chapter by brainstorming or mindmapping, and then we began to freewrite. We avoided outlining. We knew the newer techniques were more powerful. Your experiences may be different. The important point is, don't feel you're not doing it right if you don't use all these tools all the time. Use what you need when you need it.

Let's briefly describe each of the four prewriting techniques.

Brainstorming. Brainstorming lets you free-associate your ideas in random, unstructured form. Brainstorming is one of the best methods for getting your ideas on paper initially, as a releasing, free-flowing method. It's a powerful way to loosen up your tightness about writing so you can begin to create.

Suppose you had to write a letter requesting information so that your company could submit a proposal for work. Your mind is blocked and you have no way to begin. You've already used the SPEAK IT principles. You know your audience, purpose, tone, and results. Yet, you still have writer's block. What do you do?

We suggest brainstorming your ideas. Here's our brainstorm of a letter written by the ABC Corporation requesting information about the Employee Assistance Program of Floyd Consultants, Inc.

> address to pres
>
> ask purpose for info
>
> reason we need it
>
> results wanted
>
> any other info

Keep in mind that you do not necessarily have to use all these ideas and that they don't have to be in any particular order. Most people compose with two voices simultaneously competing inside them. One is the writer's voice: creative and uncensored; the other is the editor's voice: critical, judgmental, repressive. You don't want your editor to start doing the work too soon. Your editor is vital and necessary, but editing comes at the end, not at the beginning.

Mindmapping or clustering. A close cousin to brainstorming is a technique called mindmapping or clustering. Mindmapping is a visual representation of the way your mind sorts information. You start with your central thought in the middle of the page then branch your ideas off this core idea. Sometimes we refer to mindmapping as clustering because the mind clusters, or lumps, related ideas.

There is no one correct way to mindmap, but here are some general guidelines so you can start:

○ In the center of your paper, draw a square or a circle.

○ Inside it write the subject of your document.

○ Draw branches from the circle, like branches from a tree, to designate your main topics or concerns.

○ To help identify these topics, you might use the five W's and one H. Ask yourself, who, what, when, where, why, and how.

○ Branch off into smaller but related topics.

○ Don't worry about the organization of your branches — that comes later.

○ If desired, after you're finished, use different colored pens or pencils to designate related topics.

Here's our mindmap for the same letter:

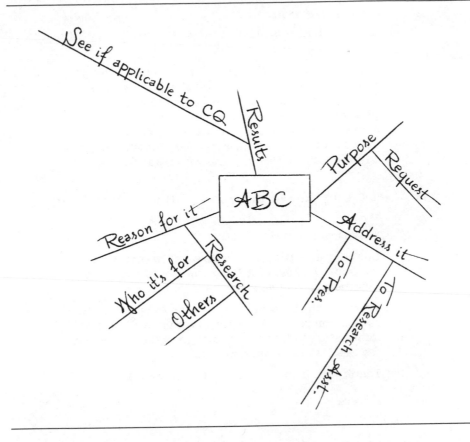

Freewriting. Freewriting is writing without an editor or a voice talking to you that wants you to edit, change, and rewrite as you compose. To freewrite, pick up your pen, or boot up your wordprocessor, and start writing. Don't make any changes or corrections, and don't start over. Ignore punctuation, spelling, grammar, and organization. Let your thoughts flow freely. You'll have time to go back later and revise them. If your thoughts wander, don't worry. Go with the flow of your mind. The important thing is to keep writing and not to stop until you have run out of ideas. Remember, you probably have your thoughts already down in your brainstorm or mindmap, although that is not necessarily a prerequisite.

Here's our freewriting exercise for our preceding letter:

> I need to ask for info on the Employee Asst. Program. It is for research so we can develop our own Asst. Program. We want a combination of all the best programs so I've got to get a lot of data. I should address this to the pres cuz we also want the president to get a taste of our company. But the secretary will probably be the only one who reads it.

Now let's jump ahead and look at the finished letter.

> Dear Mrs. Fuentes:
>
> Our company, the ABC Corporation, wants to develop an Employee Assistant Program. Would you please send us a copy of your company program?
>
> We are in the process of requesting information from several companies. We want to combine all of this information to form an effective program. Hopefully, the results will be only positive.
>
> Thank you. If we can offer help, please ask.
>
> Sincerely,
>
>
> Dina Casanova
> DC:ce

You've finished brainstorming, mindmapping, and freewriting, what do you do next? Now that you've done your groundwork, you need to organize these tools. If you're comfortable using the traditional outline, go ahead and use it. Our experience shows that writers often get bogged down in the format of outlining rather than concentrating on organizing the content. If you decide to use an outline, we suggest that you ignore format and just put your ideas in a logical, chronological order.

Another approach, which is a cousin of the outlining technique, is what we call the pyramid method. The foundation of this approach is the principle of deductive reasoning. Simply stated, you leave the most important idea for the end, building toward your climax.

The opposite of deductive reasoning is inductive reasoning. With this approach, which we call the inverted pyramid, you begin with your conclusion. Next you state how you arrived at your conclusion and why you support it.

We suggest using the inverted pyramid for all your correspondence—memos and short letters, as well as longer correspondence; for longer letters, proposals, and reports, we find the pyramid works best.

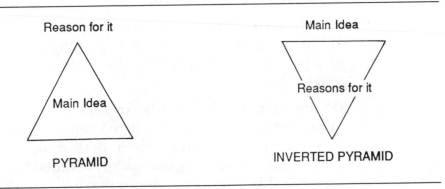

FORMAT IT

Here's where you decide how your document will look. Consider the margins, the tabs, the type of paper, the amount of white space, the indentation of paragraphs, and the block style. Also consider whether to right and left justify, or use ragged right and left justify. We find that choosing a format is an individual choice. But consistency is even more important than which format you choose.

Many companies have a style they prefer for all correspondence, especially external documentation. We suggest you find out what that format is and then use it.

If your company has no such preference and everyone seems to be using an individual format, or, if you are a new company looking for a format, we have some suggestions. In our next two chapters, we provide Westroots guidelines for formatting memos and letters. For now, here are some general Westroots guidelines for formatting all documents.

- Be consistent. All memos should have the same format. Letters should have the same format. Always adopt a format for each type of document you produce and be consistent throughout your company.

- Use block style between paragraphs, instead of indenting five spaces when beginning a new paragraph. It gives your documents a cleaner look.

- Do not right and left justify your margins; rather, left justify and use ragged right. Here is an example of a letter written both ways. The first example is right and left justified, the second is block style, with ragged right.

February 24, 1987

David Block
560 Wrightwood
Mayer, AZ 86333

Dear David:

I thought that you would like to know about two properties in your neighborhood marketed by ABC Realty, Inc.

I am happy to say that 4444 Stockton Place, a 2-bedroom/1 bath house approximately 1100 square feet, listed at $100,000, went into escrow three weeks from its being offered.

Also, 2222 Arcadia Street, a 2-bedroom/1 bath home approximately 1000 square feet, sold within 24 hours of being listed at $90,000.

If you have any questions regarding these two properties or are seriously considering the marketing of your property, please call me at 555-6000.

Sincerely,

Raymond T. Fuller

RTF:lo

February 24, 1987

David Block
560 Wrightwood
Mayer, AZ 86333

Dear David:

I thought that you would like to know about two properties in your neighborhood marketed by ABC Realty, Inc.

I am happy to say that 4444 Stockton Place, a 2-bedroom/1 bath house approximately 1100 square feet, listed at $100,000, went into escrow three weeks from its being offered.

Also, 2222 Arcadia Street, a 2-bedroom/1 bath home approximately 1000 square feet, sold within 24 hours of being listed at $90,000.

If you have any questions regarding these two properties or are seriously considering the marketing of your property, please call me at 555-6000.

Sincerely,

Raymond T. Fuller

RTF:lo

○ Use headers to break up your lengthier documents. They show the reader what topic follows, provide easy reference for later use, and give visual variety to the page. It will help the appearance of your documents, and make them easier to read or skim.

○ Use lists for easier reading and to create more white space, setting them off from the rest of the text with bullets, numbers, or letters. Generally, we suggest using numbers or letters if order is important, and bullets if it is not.

Here's an excerpt from a memo with headers and bulleted lists:

Here are instructions on how to mail a package overnight.

SIZE

You must categorize your package in three sizes:

     ○ 9 × 11.5
     ○ 9 × 13
     ○ 9 × 15.

WEIGHT

You must categorize your package in three weight divisions:

- 1/2 ounce
- 1 ounce
- 2 ounces.

○ Single-space all business correspondence, leaving double spaces between paragraphs and triple spaces between sections in longer documents.

WRITE IT

Now you're ready to write and rewrite your document. You've brainstormed, mindmapped, freewritten, organized your words, chosen your format, and you are ready! At this point, you should have a freewritten draft. Before you start, we're going to provide you with Westroots Rules of Writing. These are guidelines to keep in mind while you're writing and rewriting your first draft.

WESTROOTS RULES OF WRITING

1. Decrease sentence length.
2. Omit needless words.
3. Avoid stuffy language.
4. Use strong verbs.

These are by no means all the rules we could provide. However, we want to make your writing as simple, easy, and pleasant as possible. We believe that if you adhere to these basic principles, your writing will be clear and effective.

What follows is a brief description of Westroots Rules of Writing.

1. Decrease sentence length. We believe shorter is better. Keep your sentences to an average of twenty words. Some sentences may be only fifteen words, others may be twenty-five. Vary your sentence length, and your writing will capture your reader's attention. The shorter your sentences, the clearer and easier they are to understand. If sentences are too lengthy, they're probably confusing or frustrating to your reader.

A quick, easy way to eyeball your sentence length is to count the number of lines per sentence. An average sentence shouldn't be longer than two to three typed lines in your document. Read your sentences aloud. If you have to take a second breath before finishing, your sentence is probably too long. Also, watch for the word *and*. Writers often string two thoughts together with *and* in between. Look at this *long* sentence:

> We informed Mr. Johnstone that since our listing was in jeopardy and it looked like we were going to be terminated, it seemed somewhat ridiculous for us to hire a runner and do the mass mailing for this particular project, due to the fact that the lead time was so short and the probability of us getting a positive result from a mailing would be nil.

You get tired just trying to read this sentence, let alone understanding what this writer attempts to communicate. Here's our version:

> We informed Mr. Johnstone that since our listing was in jeopardy, it looked as if we were going to be terminated. Therefore, we decided not to hire a runner and do the mass mailing for this project.

Since the lead time was so short, it was not
practical to proceed with the mailing.

The writer of the original sentence needed more help than just shortening the sentences. We improved it by shifting a few words around and placing a period at appropriate places in the sentence. We have turned one confusing sentence into three shorter, clearer sentences.

We want to caution you from going to the other extreme. Don't write all short, choppy sentences! The key here is to vary your sentence length, keeping the longest sentences to around twenty words.

2. *Omit needless words*. Many people think that better writing requires them to reformulate and restate entire phrases, sentences, and paragraphs. In school, teachers taught us to redo, rework, rephrase, and restate. Longer was better. They were wrong! Cut out extra words as if you had a pair of scissors. When you first begin to write, it is easy to look for and delete those useless, cluttering words.

Watch out for adverbs. If your verb is strong enough, you won't need an extra word to modify it. Adverbs are easy to point out—they usually end in "ly." Here's a sentence with an overuse of adverbs.

She really wanted us to finish the job quickly so
she could look very good to our boss.

If we change the verbs and eliminate the adverbs *really*, *quickly*, and *very*, we have a stronger sentence.

She urged us to rush the job so she could impress
our boss.

Avoid excess prepositional phrases. You lose impact, and you can confuse your reader. Avoid sentences like this:

The owner of the car from the house on the corner
sold a lawnmower to the owner of the house next
to his.

Eliminate all of these prepositions, and you'll have a clearer sentence:

> The car owner from the corner house sold a
> lawnmower to his next-door neighbor.

Much improved, isn't it? Use your preposition list in the Appendix to identify these words.

Avoid using slash marks between two similar words as shown in the example that follows. Also, see if you can cut out some of the useless, unnecessary words.

> Many unprecedented discrepancies/problems were
> found/discovered and/or clearly cited in a report
> following this memo that clearly show areas
> where specific problems/difficulties occur of a
> conflicting nature.

Do your changes resemble ours?

> Many discrepancies were found and cited in the
> report attached to this memo. This report shows
> many conflicting problems.

Techniques like *discrepancies/problems*, *found/discovered*, and *problems/difficulties* create confusion and are redundant. We broke the long sentence into two short ones, using Westroots rule number one. We also removed the adverb *clearly* (used twice), and the adjectives *unprecedented*, and *specific*. We deleted the slashed marked words, *problems*, *or*, *discovered*, and *difficulties*. It's always preferable to choose one word.

The first example shows that the writer couldn't decide which word to use. Not only is the writing confusing it also makes the writer appear indecisive. The prepositional phrase *of a conflicting nature* clutters the sentence. Our revision is clearer, easy to read, and makes sense, too! Is yours?

Watch out for useless introductory phrases, such as *I think*, or *I believe*, or *she is a woman who. . . .* Read this sentence and see what you think:

> She is the woman who works for the ABC Corporation.

Wouldn't it be better to say this:

> She works for the ABC Corporation.

We know you think this way. Why else would you say it? Obviously, "she" is a woman; what else could "she" be?

Keep essential words in your sentences. Throw out the rest.

3. *Avoid stuffy language*. This rule is the cornerstone of the SPEAKWRITE system. Relax stuffy, pompous language and your correspondence will represent you as a natural and congenial person. Here's a short list of stuffy language and suggestions on how to avoid using it.

INSTEAD OF	TRY
Of a conflicting nature	Conflicts
In order to	To
As to whether	Whether
Enclosed please find	Enclosed or attached
I'm sure you can appreciate	(Avoid altogether)
At that point in time	Then
At this point in time	Now

Avoid adding "ize" to words to "dress" them up, such as:

> prioritize
>
> maximize
>
> normalize
>
> minimize
>
> utilize.

When you went to your office this morning and handed your assistant some work, did you say to him, "Enclosed please find three letters I prioritized for you." If you did, he probably gave you a strange, confused look. Most likely you said something like this: "John, here are three letters I want you to work on. Please do the most important items first."

Let's look at a few more sentences and see how we can use SPEAKWRITE to relax them:

> At this point in time I'm not sure as to whether or not I can attend the meeting.

This is better:

> Right now, I'm not sure I can make the meeting.

That is how we'd say it, so that's how we write it. Try rewording this sentence:

> I would like to thank you for your outstanding work on the MacPhillips Project.

This rewrite is less wordy and more direct:

> Thank you for your outstanding work on the MacPhillips project.

Our SPEAKWRITE revision highlights the person who did the great job instead of the person who congratulates him.

Avoid words with Latin or Greek origins. They tend to be three or four syllables, more difficult to pronounce, and more formal to the ear. Anglo-Saxon words tend to be shorter, more conventional, and easier to understand.

INSTEAD OF	TRY
implement	use
designate	show
originate	start

For additional words, check the lists of Simpler Words and Phrases in the Appendix.

Basically, we teach our business clients to use conversational words whenever possible and whenever appropriate. Of course, because of the complexity of business today, there will be times when the need for precision will require more business or technical terminology. We're not saying never to use those words. What we are saying is to remember who your audience is and try not to write to impress them; just write to communicate with them. If the more complex, technical word justifies your point and your audience knows its meaning, then use it.

4. Use strong verbs. Verbs instill power in your writing. The central word in your sentence is the verb. It's the action word, the only one that actually works for you. Most people rely on weak or inactive verbs rather than strong and active verbs when they write. Their sentences "sit" rather than "move" on the page. That's exactly the opposite of what you want to accomplish.

The two kinds of verbs are "action" and "being." Cut out all forms of the verb *to be*. For starters, eliminate *is, are, was, will be, can,* or *should*. See the Appendix for the *to be* verbs to avoid.

Look at this sentence:

> My assistant manager was helpful in assisting us
> in winning the MacPhillips Contract.

Notice the word *was*. It does nothing to enhance the sentence. Scan the sentence for the most important words. The key words in the statement are *helpful*, *assisting*, and *winning*. How does this sentence sound now?

> My assistant manager helped us win the MacPhil-
> lips Contract.

Some other frequently used verbs are weak rather than strong. But it's not possible to avoid them all the time. Stay away from using *to do, to make, to seem, to appear, to be,* and *to get.* Although all these verbs are grammatically correct, they lack power.

REFINE IT

Professional writers know that good writing requires endless rewriting. Often, people are better rewriters and editors than authors. No one should expect to turn out perfect copy the first time. However, by mastering the steps in this book, you will turn out better copy the first time. Still, this final SPEAKWRITE step, "Refine it," teaches you how to move your correspondence from ordinary to outstanding.

Refining, rewriting, polishing, and proofing are all part of the editing process. In Part One of this book, we discussed in great detail the techniques to use to refine and edit your work. However, at this point, we want to present Westroots Rules of Refining. They consist of asking yourself these questions:

- ○ Have I written to the audience that I want to address?
- ○ Have I used the appropriate tone for the people or person who's going to receive it?
- ○ Is my language appropriate for my audience? Is it natural and comfortable?
- ○ Have I proofed this document thoroughly using Westroots Rules for Proofreading:
    - ○ Let it sit.
    - ○ Read it aloud.
    - ○ Exchange it with a colleague.
    - ○ Read it backwards.
    - ○ Check referenced material.
    - ○ Make it perfect.
- ○ Have I accomplished my original purpose in writing?
- ○ Did I ask for what I want? How would I speak this?

By following Westroots Rules of Refining, you can become an objective critic of your own correspondence. Now let's apply the SPEAKWRITE System to memos.

CHAPTER 8

Writing Winning Memos

FORMATS

A MEMO—FROM START TO FINISH

REFINE IT

Memos are perhaps the most important piece of business correspondence you'll ever write. They are the most popular. Whereas some companies complain that their employees write too many memos, others complain that their employees don't write enough. Either way, memos are the most important form of interoffice correspondence. Generally, because they are internal, they're informal. Look at the following excerpt written by a project manager to her boss:

> Proposals for billing a job can be effective in improving cash flow. A detailed billing breakdown by completed activity or percent complete can be prepared before the job sold to the client then and used throughout the job to invoice with a minimum of administrative effort and maximum of "front loaded" activity values.

Can you understand what she tries to say? If so, you probably read it several times. Unfortunately, this memo typifies most business writing. It confuses, mixes ideas, and uses unnecessary jargon. In this chapter, we're going to teach you how to write an excellent memo.

Jay Fleming, a Project Manager for ABC Software, a computer software publisher, was summoned to his boss's office. His boss instructed Jay not to write any more memos. Anything Jay had to say to him, or anyone else, he could say personally. Jay knew his boss was a poor writer and hated to put anything in writing. Jay's excellent writing skills threatened to reveal his boss's poor writing skills. As a matter of fact, the boss would often coerce Jay into writing some of his memos and then signing his name to them! Unfortunately for Jay's boss the nature of ABC's work required written documents to show a project's progress. Missed deadlines resulted because of improper documentation and inappropriate blame. Eventually Jay's boss was transferred to a lower department and Jay was promoted to Division Manager. Jay's promotion probably had something to do with his careful memo writing. In addition, Jay set a good example with his memo-writing skill, and the company adopted a memo policy based on his style.

Maybe you work in a company that has a memo policy. Another company we know has a policy that memos can't be longer than one page. If anyone sends a memo longer than a page, management stamps it "unread" and sends it back to the writer. That's the way to teach brevity.

Look at the brief memo that follows. One of our clients received it as a "friendly" reminder about his W-4 form. This memo is a common type of "information" memo.

MEMORANDUM

This is to remind you that we still have not received a 1987 W-4 form from you. We've enclosed the simplified form, W-4a, and ask that you fill it out and return it to the Payroll Department as soon as possible. If you have any questions about your withholding we can supply you with a leaflet from the IRS that assists you in determining the number of exemptions you should claim.

Sincerely,

Payroll Department

This short, effective memo could be even better.

Here's our rewrite of this same memo. Pay close attention to the format:

MEMO

To: Employees with Delinquent W-4's
From: Dennis Fox, Payroll Supervisor
Date: May 15, 1987
Subject: FINAL DUE DATE OF W-4'S

We still haven't received your 1987 W-4 form. We've enclosed the new "simplified" W-4a form for your convenience.

Please return it to Payroll no later than May 31, 1987. The IRS states that if employees fail to fill out a W-4, the employer will use a standard deduction for them. This could result in heavy penalties for you at tax time.

If you have any questions about your withholding, we can supply you with a leaflet from the IRS. It helps you determine the number of exemptions you should claim. We will try to help you any way we can.

Thanks.

DF:jsm

cc: Michelle Cotter
      Accounting Director

The preceding two memos are different. They differ in tone as well as in format. The first writer hurried, and it shows. He didn't even identify himself as the Payroll Supervisor! This could make quite a difference in the results he achieves. The second uses the company format, is friendlier, and lets the readers know that Dennis Fox, the Supervisor from the Payroll Department, will help them.

The second memo sympathizes and attempts to alleviate employees' confusion and frustration. It is the better memo.

FORMATS

Before starting a memo, you need some type of format. You can use any format for memo writing you wish; however, be consistent. If no particular format exists in your company, try the format most frequently used by your top management. You might even suggest a format. The writer of the first memo in the preceding example completely ignored his company's format. The second memo reflects the Westroots' format for memo writing. It is the preferred format used by most of the companies we interviewed for this book. Let's take a closer look. We have numbered the sections of the memo for easier reference.

        (1) MEMO

(2) To: (3) Employees with Delinquent W-4's

(4) From: (5) Dennis Fox, Payroll Supervisor

(6) Date: May 15, 1987

(7) Subject: (8) FINAL DUE DATE OF W-4'S

We still haven't received your 1987 W-4 form. We've enclosed the new "simplified" W-4a form for your convenience.

(9) Please return it to Payroll no later than May 31, 1987. The IRS states that if employees fail to fill out a W-4, the employer will use a standard deduction for them. This could result in heavy penalties for you at tax time.

If you have any questions about your withholding, we can supply you with a leaflet from the IRS. It helps you

     determine the number of deductions you should claim.
     We will try to help you any way we can.

  (10) Thanks.

  (11) DF:jsm

  (12) cc: Michelle Cotter
       Accounting Director

Following this paragraph are the reasons for each phase of this memo. If you follow these easy steps every time, you'll have a perfectly formatted memo. It will be a great reflection on you.

1. To distinguish this correspondence from any other, type "MEMO" at the top of the page. *Memo* is a more contemporary and relaxed word than the more formal word *Memorandum. Memo* also reflects the informality of the correspondence.

2. Use "To" as the first of your identification lines. This line comes first because your audience is the most important aspect of your communication.

3. This line refers to the main people who will receive and take action on your memo. Additional interested or concerned individual(s) are listed below under "cc."

4. Use "From" as the second of your identification lines to identify yourself as the writer.

5. Here, make sure you identify yourself by name. A department can't write a memo, but a department supervisor can. Plus, you should be proud to have your name on this memo!

6. The date is important so that the reader recognizes the urgency of the memo and the time when you wrote it. In our first example, no one knows the

date of the memo, or the time when the W-4s are due. Both are crucial for this subject matter.

7. Use "Subject" rather than "Re," "Reference," or "Regarding." "Subject" is more contemporary, and we don't use "Re" in speech.

8. Make your subject as specific, concise, and appealing as you can. Although it is often difficult to do when dealing with unpleasant topics, it is a way to attract your reader to your subject. Capitalize each letter to attract attention. Your assistant can also use the subject line for filing purposes. Make the subjects as appealing and attention-grabbing as you can. Bland subject heads lose readers; spicy ones attract them. After all, you don't want your memo to wind up in the circular file.

9. The dominant trend in today's paragraph formatting tends toward the block style format; the copy is typed flush left and ragged right. Our second memo is an example of the block style format. Avoid the temptation, if writing on a word processor, to justify the right margin. The writing is more difficult to read and comprehend, if you justify both left and right margins. Our first memo example is right and left justified. Even though most published books are right and left justified, the business trend has moved away from this rigid format. The Westroots' method prefers block style and ragged right margins for everyday business correspondence.

    Headers are equivalent to subheads in a newspaper and help to divide long memos into shorter topics. Although our preceding two examples do not use headers, because of their brevity, the longer memo on pages 121–122 does. Headers help to break up lengthy text, show the reader what topic follows, provide easy reference for later use, and give visual variety to the page. Use judgment with headers, but if your memo's appearance and content improve with them, go ahead.

10. Salutation and signature lines are not necessary in memos. Sometimes, however, the writer will initial the memo before it circulates to show approval of the content.

11. This line provides the initials in upper case of the writer followed by a colon and the initials in lower case of the typist or word processor. If you've typed the memo yourself, no initials are necessary.

12. The "cc" refers to "carbon copy." In today's technological age of computers, word processors, and laser printers, carbon copies are an endangered species. However, duplicated copies are not. Thus "cc" is still the acceptable abbreviation for who else, besides the primary recipients, will receive copies. In this case, the Director of Accounting will receive a copy. Directing a copy to her informs her that you are doing your job and following up on the W-4 problem. Also, it may help your readers respond faster if they know the "Director" received a copy. Another consideration when using "cc" is the order of the recipients. Many companies have adopted the order of management: top managers first, mid-level managers second, and so on. Westroots suggests the alphabetical format. That way, you don't have to keep an organizational chart in front of you when you write anything, including memos, letters, and reports. Also, it makes your business life easier, and it helps you avoid making a disastrous political error. In our memo, since only the Director of Accounting was "cc-ed," that was not a problem. In our next example, let's see what the writer does.

A MEMO—FROM START TO FINISH

The following example is from one of our clients, Patrick Kearny, a project manager for an engineering firm on the West Coast. The company decided to upgrade their computers. If any project managers wanted a new personal computer, they had to write a memo justifying why they needed one.

How did Patrick handle this task? He felt overwhelmed by it. First, he talked to some technical people in his company and obtained technical and background information. Then he came to us with this first draft. We thought it was a good first attempt. However, we were able to improve it quite a bit. Here is Patrick's first draft:

INTEROFFICE MEMORANDUM

To: Doug Preston
From: Patrick Kearny
Date: May 26, 1987
Subject: COMPUTER PURCHASE FOR
           NATIONAL DIVISION

Division personnel need a computer primarily as a project management tool. The software requested plus already available software would improve our ability to plan projects, control project finances, and automate record keeping. The technical nature of our projects and the sophistication of our clients demand that we improve our capabilities.

This request includes word processing software. However, with only one modern computer available to the division, it would be better not to tie up the machine with something the ABC 50 can do adequately. On the other hand, the ABC 50 is inadequate for all the other needs discussed in this memo.

Interoffice Memorandum (Cont.)

I. Project Planning

   A. Software
      1. PMS II
      2. PERT +

   B. Comment: Until a program is blessed as "the company" software, I recommend having both programs available.

   C. How better project planning makes money:
      1. The act of producing a CPM of PERT schedule can give a manager a better understanding of the project and how to build it most efficiently.
      2. A manager can be more confident of project cash flow if the expenses are based on an accurate schedule.

II. Financial Management

   A. Software
      1. Lotus 1-2-3

   B. Comment: Software for preparing change orders would be helpful, but none seem to be available.

   C. How playing "what if" makes money:
      1. Setting up or modifying the project management summary (PMS) is most effectively done when immediate feedback is available to the manager as he makes the changes.
      2. Proposals for billing a job can be effective in improving cash flow. A detailed billing breakdown by completed activity or percent complete can be prepared before the job, sold to the client then and used throughout the job to invoice with a minimum of administrative effort and maximum of "front loaded" activity values.
         2.1 Positive cash flow is more likely when this type of invoicing is based on an accurate expense flow developed from a good schedule.
         2.2 This type of invoicing minimizes time spent with the client arguing about the validity of the invoice.

2.3 Preparing this type of invoice on a
microcomputer minimizes the time
spent preparing the initial invoicing
proposal as well as the time spent
each month preparing the invoice.
3. A computerized spread sheet permits
faster setup and changing of divisional
and other budgets.

III. Data Management
A. Software
1. D Base III
B. How sortable, printable lists make money:
1. There are several advantages to putting
the various lists we use on a computer
first instead of directly on a piece
of paper.
2. The computer can provide a system for
neatly organizing and presenting the
information.
Examples are:

- o Drawing Logs
- o Letter Subject and Serial Number Files
- o Requests for Engineering Information
(REI's)
- o Change Orders
- o Change Estimates
- o Purchase Orders
- o Marketing Leads.

3. With a Xerox machine available, logs, or
parts of them, can be immediately
distributed, included in reports, or sent
to clients without the need to retype or
use blueprint machines.
4. Well organized, complete, and legible
information can be critical to the successful preparation of a claim.

Some of the problems in Patrick's approach are:

○ His memo is too long. He needs to make his point in as few words as possible. Remember the one-page memo policy? It might be difficult to limit this memo to one page. But, it's important to say what you have to say briefly, clearly, and concisely.

○ Although he made an attempt to be organized, we found his organization confusing. Using heads and subheads would have been easier to follow than his complicated numbering system.

○ There is no conclusion or summary paragraph. He should sum up his ideas briefly in a short paragraph especially since the memo is so long. Remember, you should let your readers know what you expect from them.

We suggested he mindmap his ideas and then follow the company's guidelines. First, we sat down with him and went through a quick Speak It exercise. We asked him these questions, and after some coaching, we came up with the following answers:

Who is your audience?

> My boss, Doug Preston, Executive Vice-President. Also, if Doug approves the request, it will pass to the Director of the Information Services Division, who makes the final decision.

What is your purpose?

> My immediate purpose is to get Doug to approve my memo, and pass it on to Information Services. Ultimately, of course, I want Information Services to approve the purchase of the computer.

What is your tone?

Positive, confident, assertive. That's what I want it to
say. I'm not sure the memo gets that across. It isn't
clear, is it?

What is your desired result from sending this memo?

To get Information Services to approve the purchase
of a personal computer dedicated to my project.

Here's the mindmap that emerged:

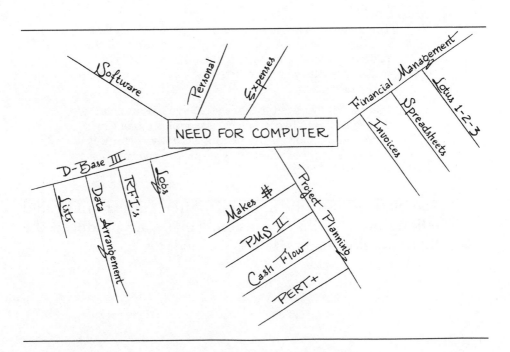

After we finished mindmapping, we helped Patrick organize his ideas in order of importance, putting the most important items first.

After all of this, Patrick freewrote the following memo.

> Let's see, I want to write about three areas: Project Planning, Financial Management, Data Management, and I want to give some financial examples. Wow, and in only two pages, max! How am I ever going to do that??? Also I want to organize it better. And make it less wordy.
>
> I better leave out the stuff about word processing software. I think that diverts me from the main issue here.
>
> Ok here goes: Project Planning. I can talk about how better project planning helps the company to make money and give a brief example.
>
> Then I can talk about Financial Management, especially Lotus 1-2-3, since that is the software we all want to use. How a spreadsheet will permit fast set up and budget analysis.
>
> Then there's data management, especially mentioning that we want to use D Base III and can't on the present computer system. D Base III will help us make sortable, printable lists and how that will help make us money.
>
> I think I'll leave out all that stuff about Financial Examples and "hypothetical" examples since I'm supposed to shorten the memo. Actually, I think it'll be good enough without it. I think I'm ready to get in there and WRITE!

Patrick then wrote the first draft. After a little refining and editing he added a conclusion. Finally, he produced the following document. He was pleased.

MEMO

To: Doug Preston
From: Patrick Kearny
Date: May 26, 1987
Subject: COMPUTER PURCHASE FOR
            NATIONAL DIVISION

Division personnel need an IBM Compatible Personal
Computer as a project management tool. Available
software improves our ability to plan project finances
and automate record keeping. The technical nature of
our projects and the sophistication of clients demand
we improve our capabilities.

PROJECT PLANNING—PMS II AND PERT +

○ A CPM of a PERT schedule gives a manager a
complete understanding of the project and
how to build it.

○ An accurate schedule helps a manager to be
more confident of project cash flow.

○ Critical path analysis keeps management's
attention focused on the critical activities.

○ A well thought-out schedule network is an
excellent communication tool. Many clients
now require such a schedule.

FINANCIAL MANAGEMENT—LOTUS 1-2-3

○ The project manager requires immediate
feedback as he sets up or modifies the project
management summary (PMS).

○ Proposals for billing jobs are effective in
improving cash flow. Billing breakdowns by
completed activities can be prepared before
the job and sold to the client. These breakdowns help throughout the job in efficient
invoicing with minimal administrative effort.

DATA MANAGEMENT—D BASE III

○ We can produce sortable, printable lists for organizing and presenting information. Examples are:

  ○ Drawing Logs
  ○ Letter Subject and Serial Number Files
  ○ Requests for Engineering Information (REI's)
  ○ Change Orders
  ○ Change Estimates
  ○ Purchase Orders
  ○ Marketing Leads.

○ We can immediately distribute logs or include them in reports to clients.

○ We can prepare successful claims with organized, complete, and legible data.

In summary, an IBM compatible computer is a necessity for the project manager's efficiency and effectiveness on his projects. It provides him with the necessary backup documentation and ultimately increases company profits.

Notice the new organization of the memo. It is cleaner, uses headings and subheadings, and generally has an overall professional look. By the way, there is a postscript to this story. Doug approved Patrick's request. Information Services agreed that Patrick's project deserved a personal computer. Patrick won approval not only because of the arguments he raised in his memo, but because it was well-organized, well-thought out, and well-written. Patrick says the SPEAKWRITE system helped him, and he now relies on it often.

The following memo is an example of a courtesy memo. The writer is informing her staff of a personal change within the company. See if you can use SPEAK-WRITE to rewrite it. Work on the cold, impersonal tone and try to add some warmth to your version. Don't move on to the next page until you've completed your rewrite. Then you can compare it with our suggested revision.

Try rewriting this memo:

MEMO

To:	Distribution
From:	Gail Neimetz
Date:	May 26, 1987
Subject:	PROMOTION

We are announcing the promotion of Phyllis Spencer to the position of Technical AVP reporting to Peter Velasquez within the ABC branch of Engineering. Phyllis, in her previous position as Commercial Systems Director in Larry Birmingham's business group, has served most-recently as Technical Director of the CBM Program. She has contributed significantly to the success of the CBM program during her 3 years of involvement, and will continue her role there while gradually becoming more-broadly involved in ABC engineering activities.

Phyllis joined ABC Communications in 1985, after concluding 6 years of employment with The Boeing Company as General Manager of their San Francisco division. During 3 years of prior employment with the Electric Corporation, she held a number of technical positions, including that of Manager with the company's Technology branch. Phyllis earned her Ph.D in communications/control theory at Stanford University and spent 8 years with Philips Radio engaged in communications-system design/analysis and project engineering. She is a patentee in her field and has authored 10 technical publications.

Please support Phyllis in her new engineering role.

Maybe your revised memo looks something like this:

MEMO

To: Everyone
From: Gail Neimetz
Date: May 26, 1987
Subject: PROMOTION

Let's congratulate our Phyllis Spencer on her promotion to Technical AVP. She will report to Peter Velasquez in the ABC branch of Engineering.

Phyllis was previously Commercial Systems Director in Larry Birmingham's business group. Recently, she served as Technical Director of the CBM Program. She contributed significantly to the success of the CBM project during her three years there. She will continue her role there while gradually becoming more involved in ABC engineering activities.

Phyllis joined ABC Communications in 1985, after six years of employment with The Boeing Company as General Manager of their San Francisco division. During three years of employment with the Electric Corporation, she held a number of technical positions, including Manager with the company's Technology branch.

Phyllis earned her Ph.D in communications/control theory at Stanford University. She spent eight years with Philips Radio working in communications system design/analysis and project engineering. In addition, she is a patentee in her field and has authored ten technical publications.

Let's welcome Phyllis in her new engineering role and give her our support.

There's not just one way to approach the document. But did you consider your audience, purpose, tone, and results? Go over the elements discussed in our last chapter. Check out your format. Does it follow your company's or the suggested SPEAKWRITE format? If you feel satisfied, then you've probably written a clear, concise, and friendly courtesy memo.

REFINE IT

You aren't finished until you use Westroots rules of refining and proofing discussed in the SPEAKWRITE chapter. Here are some additional techniques for refining your memos before they leave your desk:

- Keep in mind Westroots basic principle of good writing. Write the way you speak— conversationally and naturally.

- Avoid needless words and unnecessary jargon.

- Write with short sentences and paragraphs.

- Use lists and headings.

- Use strong action verbs. Watch *to be* verbs. Use the action verb lists.

- Simple is strongest. Where possible, substitute short words and everyday language.

- Use smooth transitions between paragraphs. Use the transition word list.

- Use active voice. Read more about active and passive voice in Part One.

- If you must use passive voice, use it concisely and selectively. Use it for emphasis or when you purposely intend to be vague.

○ Ask yourself these questions:

  ○ Have I addressed my intended audience?
  ○ Is my purpose clearly stated?
  ○ Is my tone friendly and positive?
  ○ Do I tell my reader what I want done?
  ○ Finally, proof your memo one last time using Westroots Proofing Techniques.

Now, on to letters. . . .

CHAPTER 9

Producing Powerful Letters

SPEAK IT

PLAN IT

FORMAT IT

WRITE IT

REFINE IT

Your business letters are about important issues. Next to memos, they are probably the most important documents you have to write. These letters provide good and bad news, ask and answer questions, ask for and give credit, sell to and persuade people, and make and adjust complaints.

When and how do you write these letters? You write them in almost the same way as you write memos.

SPEAK IT

You can use the SPEAKWRITE system as effectively with letters as you do with memos. Consider your:

- ○ Audience
- ○ Tone
- ○ Purpose
- ○ Results.

Look at the following letter one of our clients brought to us for some help.

April 14, 1987

San Diego Construction Co.
5849 Ocean Way
San Diego, California 92101

Attention: Mr. Marshall Hall

Subject: First Ocean Way — Job #8500

Dear Marshall:

I am writing to thank you and the people of San
Diego Construction Co. including especially Mr.
Philip Hardy for your role in helping make First
Ocean Way a successful condominium project.

Now that the construction phase of the project is
completed, I would like to rearrange the business
relationship between our companies. The ABC
Company would like to look to San Diego Construction for help in two areas: (1) making modifications
for the operating division, and (2) performing
warranty work for the construction division. I am
asking that before performing work, your people
determine which division is to receive and pay the
invoice. Mr. Joseph Kychik of the Operating Division
can be reached at telephone number 619-555-5000.
He can explain how invoices should be sent to the
Operating Division. Invoices for construction warranty work can be sent to the ABC Company P.O. Box
as they presently are.

San Diego Construction Co.
Attention: Mr. Marshall Hall
Subject: First Ocean Way

April 14, 1987
Page Two

In order to institute a measure of control over
warranty expenses, I am requesting that San Diego
Construction obtain a warranty work order number
from Mr. Kychik before performing warranty work.
He will obtain the number from my office.

I have advised our construction accounting department to return any invoices received for work
performed on or after April 13, 1987, unless the
warranty work order numbers appear on the face of
the invoice. Additionally, each time sheet, equipment
sheet, and material invoice must contain the warranty work order number for which it applies. This is
a little different from your present system which
describes the work done in words alone.

I will certainly appreciate the attention that you, Phil
Hardy, and Sheila O'Neal can give to make this
system work. I am sure it will help us process your
invoices faster, since the need to decipher what was
done and which division is responsible for it will be
eliminated.

Very truly yours,
ABC Company

Barbara A. Francis
Project Manager
JAL/jss

cc: P. Hardy
     J. Kychik
     S. O'Neal
     H. White
     J. Forbes
     M. Floyd
     C. Miller

It's hard to tell from what Barbara wants from Marshall
Hall after reading this letter. Barbara told us she and her

assistant spent several hours on this letter rewriting, editing, and proofreading. It mildly satisfied her—until she learned about SPEAKWRITE. Then she applied the SPEAKWRITE standards to her letter, and her flaws became apparent.

Here are some of our critiques of this letter.

- Barbara buries the purpose of the letter in the second paragraph. She wants San Diego Construction to send their invoices to the correct ABC Construction Company division and to use warranty numbers on their invoices.

- Unnecessary information clutters the letter. She presents facts San Diego Construction doesn't need to know.

- It's too long; the wordiness and jargon can be cut.

- The tone is too formal, and it patronizes the reader. The phrases "Mr. Joseph Kychik" and "your people" exemplify this patronizing tone.

- She should list the main points with headers or bullets.

- What does Barbara want Marshall Hall to do? She states the result, but it's unclear.

- She tries to write the letter to more people than Marshall Hall, such as Philip Hardy and Sheila O'Neal. She should send them individual letters.

Now, let's take a closer look at this letter.

AUDIENCE

The audience is Marshall Hall. Barbara makes a mistake also in thanking Phil Hardy and addressing Sheila O'Neal in this letter. She should send a separate letter of thanks to Phil and to Sheila. It is more polite and courteous. But just to send copies to these people isn't enough. Everyone appreciates a personal thank-you. How would you feel if you received a duplicated thank-you note?

TONE

The tone is too formal. It is almost insulting to the reader. We know Barbara means to be polite, but look at the phrases "the people of San Diego Construction," "Mr. Philip Hardy," "Mr. Joseph Kychik," and "your people." She should say, "your company," "Philip Hardy," "Joseph Kychik," and "you." It's friendlier and promotes a more helpful attitude.

PURPOSE

Barbara muddies the purpose. Is she thanking San Diego Construction, or is she asking them to send their invoices to the proper division? Is it to get San Diego Construction to obtain warranty numbers and to attach them to their invoices? The purpose should be stated clearly in the beginning of the letter. Just as in a memo, you use the inverted pyramid style. Always put your purpose or reason for the letter first, then provide the facts afterwards.

RESULTS

Barbara wants San Diego Construction to change its invoicing methods to get paid faster. But what *exactly* does Barbara want Marshall to do? This part is unclear.

PLAN IT

With a careful look at the SPEAK IT principles, we had Barbara freewrite a new letter. Here's her freewriting sample. Notice how she lets her mind wander. That's part of the freewriting technique.

April 14, 1987

San Diego Construction Co., Inc.
5849 Ocean Way
San Diego, California 92101

Attention: Mr. Marshall Hall
Reference: Job #8500
Subject: First Ocean Way

Dear Marshall:

Now why am I writing? Oh, yes, to get you to change the way you bill us so we can pay you on time. Now how do I say that clearly? Let's see, I'm supposed to use Westroots rules of writing and use shorter sentences, avoid cliches, and avoid jargon. Ok, folks here goes. . . .

I want to rearrange the business relationship between our companies. The ABC Company would like to look to San Diego Construction for help in two areas: Let's see, it might help to use bullets here.

○ making modifications for the operating division.

○ performing warranty work for the construction division.

Before sending your invoices, indicate which ABC Company is to receive and pay the invoice. Joseph Kychik of the Operating Division, 619-550-5000, can tell you how Operating Division invoices should be sent. This should be a new paragraph I think. Maybe it can be deleted. Ok, let's do it.

Construction warranty invoices will continue to go to the ABC Company P.O. Box. Well, maybe I didn't delete it, but I rewrote it instead. Please obtain a work order number from Joseph Kychik of the Operating Division before you begin any warranty work.

I have advised our construction accounting department to return any invoices received for work performed on or after April 13, 1987 unless the warranty work order numbers appear on the face of the invoice. Additionally, each time sheet, equipment sheet, and material invoice must contain the warranty work order number for which it applies.

San Diego Construction Co., Inc.
Attention: Mr. Marshall Hall
Subject: First Ocean Way
April 14, 1987
Page Two

Thanks for all your help in making our new system
work. We are looking forward to working with you in
the near future. How's that? I cut that last paragraph!

Very truly yours,
ABC Company

Barbara A. Francis
Project Manager
JAL/jss

cc: P. Hardy
     J. Kychik
     S. O'Neal
     H. White
     J. Forbes
     M. Floyd
     C. Miller

Barbara enjoyed her freewriting. It unleashed her
mind; her ideas flowed. Now let's examine the final rewrite. Notice the changes in the format. We'll discuss them
later in this chapter.

April 14, 1987

San Diego Construction Co., Inc.
5849 Ocean Way
San Diego, CA 92101

Attention: Mr. Marshall Hall, Vice President,
             Operations
Reference: Job #8500
SUBJECT: CHANGES IN OUR INVOICING
             PROCEDURES

Dear Marshall:

Thanks for making the First Ocean Way Condominium project the success that it was. So that you can receive payments on time, we have decided to change our billing procedures.

The benefits will outweigh any preliminary inconveniences.

Let me briefly list the new procedures that will affect San Diego Construction:

- ○ Send all invoices to the proper ABC Division.
- ○ Continue to send construction warranty invoices to the ABC Company P.O. Box.
- ○ Obtain a work order number from Joseph Kychik (619) 555-5000 before you begin any warranty work.
- ○ List warranty work order numbers on time sheets, equipment sheets, and material invoices.

Our accounting department informed me today that it will return any invoices received for work performed on or after April 13, 1987, unless the warranty work order numbers appear on the face of the invoice.

San Diego Construction Company
Page 2

Thanks for your help in making our new system
work. Proper use of the system will prompt quick
payment.

I look forward to working with you again in the near
future.

Sincerely,

Barbara A. Francis
Project Manager
ABC COMPANY
JAL/jss

cc: M. Floyd
     J. Forbes
     P. Hardy
     J. Kychik
     C. Miller
     S. O'Neal
     H. White

Notice how we stated the purpose in the beginning. We
also shortened both the sentences and the paragraphs and
then listed the procedures for Marshall to follow. The
letter is now clear, easy-to-read, and to the point. Will
Marshall respond positively to Barbara's request? He will if
he wants his money faster!

FORMAT IT

If your company doesn't have a standard format, or if you
are looking for a change, Westroots preferred format for
letter writing will work for you.

However, before we discuss the inside format, let's talk briefly about the look of letters in general: the stationery, the letterhead, and the overall style.

STATIONERY AND LETTERHEAD

The quality of your paper and the type of letterhead project your company's image. You probably already have good quality paper and standard letterhead. If yours is a small company, or you've just gone into business for yourself, one of the first things you must do is to invest in printing your letterhead. Use high quality bond paper with matching printed, preaddressed envelopes. The letterhead may include any symbol or emblem that identifies or describes your company. It should also include:

○ *Name of Your Company:* The name of your company should tell what you do. If it doesn't, it's fine to add a descriptive phrase that provides this information. For example, if your company is an accounting firm, and you call yourself The ABC Company of California, you could add the phrase, "Tax Accounting and Auditing" beneath the company name.

○ *Location:* This should include address, or P.O. Box, telex number, and phone number.

○ *Simplicity:* Don't clutter your stationery. Remember, the more white space on a page, the easier it is to read, the more attractive it looks, and the easier it is to remember.

○ *Optional Descriptive Information:* This can include officers and partners. Just don't include excessive information.

LETTER STYLE

If your company has a standard format, follow it. If not, we suggest block style, the same style we recommend for memos. It's cleaner and easier to read. Letters, like memos, should be single-spaced, double-spaced between paragraphs, left justified and ragged right. (See the SPEAK-WRITE chapter for more information about left justified and ragged right.) The most important thing is consistency, especially when there is frequent correspondence with the same outside agency or client. Here is an example of a block style letter using the Westroots preferred format:

April 3, 1987

Computer Applications Incorporated
2500 Industrial Drive
North Hollywood, CA 91330

Attention: Mr. Steven McDonald,
            President
Reference: CBT Training Program

Dear Steve:

As you requested during our meeting of February 23, 1987, I have enclosed the following materials:

     ○ A copy of the revised contract

     ○ A copy of the initial proposal

     ○ A sample of our Alphawriter Training Manual.

I look forward to working with you. Please call me if you have any questions.

Sincerely,

Marianne P. Floyd
Assistant Vice President
ABC Computer Company

cc: J. Bealstein
     R. Roberts

LETTER FORMAT—THE INSIDES

Let's take a closer look at the format of ABC's letter to San Diego Construction Company. Notice that we've numbered the sections so that we can easily refer to the format.

(1) April 14, 1987

(2) San Diego Construction Co., Inc.
5849 Ocean Way
San Diego, CA 92101

(3) Attention: Mr. Marshall Hall, Vice President, Operations

(4) Reference: Job #8500

(5) SUBJECT: CHANGES IN OUR INVOICING PROCEDURES

(6) Dear Marshall:

(7) Thanks for making the First Ocean Way Condominium project the success that it was. So that you can receive payments on time, we have decided to change our billing procedures. The benefits will outweigh any preliminary inconveniences.

Let me briefly list the new procedures that will affect San Diego Construction:

- Send all invoices to the proper ABC Division.
- Continue to send construction warranty invoices to the ABC Company P.O. Box.
- Obtain a work order number from Joseph Kychik (619) 555-5000 before you begin any warranty work.
- List warranty work order numbers on time sheets, equipment sheets, and material invoices.

(13) San Diego Construction Company
Page Two

Our accounting department informed me today that
it will return any invoices received for work performed on or after April 13, 1987, unless the warranty work order numbers appear on the face of the
invoice.

Thanks for your help in making our new system
work. Proper use of the system will prompt quick
payment. I look forward to working with you again
in the near future.

(8) Sincerely,

(9) Barbara A. Francis
Project Manager
ABC COMPANY
(10) JAL/jss
(11) Encl.
(12) cc: M. Floyd
J. Forbes
P. Hardy
J. Kychik
C. Miller
S. O'Neal
H. White

1. Space the date in the upper left-hand corner
   directly below the letterhead. Allow four spaces
   before the beginning of your inside address. Write
   out the date, rather than (4/14/87).

2. Include the name of the company, the address, city,
   state, and zip code. Generally, the only allowable
   abbreviations are the ones we've used: Mr., Mrs.,
   Ms., and CA (the state). We've already discussed
   abbreviations in our previous sections. Follow those
   guidelines for your inside addresses.

3. The attention line should be directed to the person who is most likely to take action on your information. If you use an attention line to designate a person or people, delete the name or names from your inside and envelope addresses. Using it in both places is redundant.

4. The reference line is used to provide job numbers, dates of previous meetings, or other material the writer needs to document. This line often takes the place of repetitious, statistical information ("This letter concerns our July 12 meeting.") in the first line of a letter.

5. The subject line is similar to the subject line in your memos. We've indicated this line with the word "Subject." This is a very important part of your letter, and every business letter should have a subject line. As with memos, your subject line should be specific, concise, and appealing. Although it may be difficult when dealing with unpleasant topics, it's a vehicle to let your reader know the content of your letter. It should grab your reader's attention; after all, that is what you want—to get your letter noticed.

6. The salutation addresses the person stated in your inside address or in your attention line. Make your greeting personal, or more formal depending on your relationship with the addressee. Use your judgment. Instead of "Dear Sir" or "Dear Mr. Hall," use "Dear (first name)." Establish some personal contact before you use first names, but always use names. Yet, if you already know someone by first name and you still want to show respect, use a title (Mr., Ms., Dr.). "Gentlemen," "Dear Sir or Madam," "To Whom It May Concern," "Dear Resident," or

"Occupant" are out! These impersonal and disinterested salutations turn away interest. They also show your lack of preparation. If you write a sales letter, take the time to find out the names of your clients. If you apply for a job, learn the name of the person who would be hiring you. If you do, you'll increase your chances of getting the job. If you bid a contract, find out the name of the people in power. If you can't find out an individual's name, address the person by the position title, such as: "Dear Personnel Manager," "Dear Alumni Association President," or "Dear Office Manager."

7. Single-space the content of your letter and double-space between paragraphs. This is consistent with our memo format. As with memos, use lists as often as you can. This technique allows the reader to grasp the important points quickly. Try not to make your letters longer than one page. If this is impossible, two pages is maximum. The closing paragraph contains a brief summary and another thanks if appropriate. Avoid cliché-filled phrases such as "If you have any questions, please don't hesitate to call." Don't tell people to call you unless you want to hear from them. If you do want them to call, leave your number and an extension, especially if it's different from the one on your letterhead. If you don't want the person to call, use statements such as "I think this letter answers all your questions," or "I trust this information clarifies your confusion." This discourages phone calls and closes the issue.

8. We vote for "Sincerely" as a closing. Other possibilities include, "Yours truly," "Regards," and "Very truly yours." Avoid being overly friendly with closings such as "Warmest regards," "Our sincere

regards," or "Best wishes." Reserve these closings for your close associates. Make the close fit the nature of the relationship. If you aren't "Very truly theirs," don't say it!

9. Place the signature four spaces below the closing. It lines up with the left margin. Sign your name on one line with your title directly under your name. The four spaces allow plenty of room for your signature. Sign every letter you write. If you are not available, and it's urgent that the letter go out, it's permissible to have someone else sign for you with the signer's initials on the side. We've placed the company name underneath Barbara's name and title. This practice is open to preference. If you have a company logo and letterhead, it might seem redundant. However, some large companies prefer to indicate the company's name so they can avoid confusion, especially if there is a parent company with several subsidiaries.

10. These uppercase initials indicate the writer of the letter, and the lowercase initials indicate the typist or the word processor.

11. Indicate an enclosure or attachment under the initials. "Encl." is an appropriate abbreviation to use.

12. The "cc" is the acceptable abbreviation for people who receive copies of your letter. In this case, seven people will receive a copy of this letter. We used the Westroots alphabetical format in listing the "cc" receivers, to avoid any misunderstandings.

13. The second page should be on a plain piece of stationery, without letterhead, or a modified letterhead. The date appears at the top followed by the page number. Space down about four spaces,

and begin your new paragraph. If possible, try to break your pages between paragraphs instead of within a paragraph.

WRITE IT

When writing your letters, use Westroots Rules of Letter Writing. In this letter, we've used the following Westroots rules:

○ Place the most important ideas in the beginning of the letter.

○ Present the main ideas with headings. Itemize subtopics in lists, using bullets. Use numbers if order of importance is relevant.

○ Personalize the letter with personal pronouns, such as *we*, *our*, and *I*.

○ Use short sentences and short paragraphs.

○ Use the active rather than passive voice. Instead of "Invoices for construction warranty work can be sent to," use "Send invoices for construction warranty work to."

○ Use strong openings and closings. Avoid empty, overused expressions such as "Enclosed please find . . . ," "Per our telephone conversation today . . . ," "According to our records, your account . . . ," "If you have any questions, please advise . . . ," "I would appreciate your attention to this matter at your earliest convenience," or the worst, "Thanking you in advance. . . ." Remember, you wouldn't talk that way to someone, so why write that way?

Now let's look at the types of business letters you write and some guidelines to follow.

GOOD-NEWS LETTERS

Good-news letters are basically that—letters that provide positive news. They award jobs, contracts, grants, requests, promotions, or make special commendations. These letters are enjoyable. We all like imparting good news. Here are Westroots rules for good-news letters. Place each of these items in a separate paragraph.

- Begin the letter with the Congratulations. Make your message positive!

- Show why you're happy. How does it help you, your company, and your employees? Be specific. You want to convince your reader you mean what you say.

- Provide any qualifications. These are the "ifs" and "buts." When you award a contract to someone, state the major stipulations or changes. For example, if you've just offered someone a promotion and ten-hour days go with the promotion, this is the place to state that qualification.

- State the results you expect. What do you want your reader to do to accept your offer? Sign a contract? Call you? Answer you with a letter? Tell your reader what you want.

○ Close the letter by briefly restating the good
  news. Reiterate your happiness.

Here is an example of a good-news letter:

> April 14, 1987
>
> San Diego Construction Co., Inc.
> 5849 Ocean Way
> San Diego, CA 92101
>
> Attention: Mr. John Walker, President
>
> Dear John:
>
> Congratulations on being awarded the First Ocean
> Way Condominium project! The competition was
> tough. It was a difficult decision, but we feel we've
> picked the best company for the job!
>
> Let's schedule a meeting to launch the project. It'll
> be a nice way for our companies to meet.
>
> Let me know when it's convenient. Thursday is good
> for us. I'm looking forward to working with you and
> San Diego Construction.
>
> Sincerely,
>
>
> J. P. Forbes
> President
> ABC Company
>
> JPP/jss
>
> cc: M. Floyd
>   C. Miller
>   H. White

BAD-NEWS LETTERS

Bad-news letters contain negative information. They're
difficult to write. These are the letters we often postpone

and sometimes *never* quite get around to writing. Examples of bad-news letters include rejections of job applicants, proposals, promotions, or manuscripts. In writing a bad-news letter, be clear on your decision without being cruel or hostile, but be firm and decisive. Let the reader know your decision is final to prevent making phone calls to you.

Here are Westroots Rules of Bad-News Letters:

○ Open with praise. "Praise before criticism" is the motto of sensitive and successful managers of the 80s. Begin your bad-news letters by using this technique. Let your reader know you care, and acknowledge that you understand the reader's problem.

○ State your decision — concisely, to the point, and firmly. Don't leave room for doubt. Be kind and gentle at the same time. Tone is extremely important in this type of letter. Never be hostile; instead be sensitive, warm, and caring.

○ State your reasons. You may be able to include this information in the preceding paragraph. Again, be kind, gentle, but firm. Let the reader know your decision was difficult.

○ Follow up with further explanations and any alternatives. For example, if you're rejecting a job applicant, encourage the person to apply for other job openings in the future. In this paragraph, make your reader feel better without offering false hope.

One friend relates his reaction to his first rejection letter from a major publisher. The negativity of the letter devastated him so much that he actually gave up writing for an entire year! Finally, he submitted a second manuscript to another publisher. Although that publisher rejected him too, the letter he received was positive. He felt encouraged and optimistic. He kept writing. Today he is a successfully published author.

o Close on a positive note. Don't repeat the bad news. Offer best wishes and tell your reader that you sincerely hope things work out.

Here is an example of a well-written bad-news letter:

September 1, 1987

Mr. Jack Fielding
6785 North Spauling Avenue
San Francisco, CA 94545

Dear Mr. Fielding:

We have received your application for the Project Manager position at the ABC Company. We have reviewed your background against our current needs. Although you have excellent qualifications, we have filled the position with someone who has more directly related experience.

We are continuing to grow and, therefore, opportunities more directly related to your background may arise in the future. We have found your background of sufficient interest, and we encourage you to apply for other openings as they occur.

In the meantime, we wish you well in your job search and thank you for your interest in the ABC Company.

Sincerely,

Josephine V. Thomas
Vice President
Human Resources Department

JVT/jss

SALES LETTERS

These letters belong in the category of persuasive communications. Every organization must sell something to survive. At one time or another, it is likely that you will have to write a sales letter.

You need to capture your reader's attention, keep it, and get your reader to do something — to take some action.

March 10, 1988

Ms. Westland
31-A Via Canter
Encinitas, CA 92017

Dear Ms. Westland:

Safe Security is no longer in business.

Any agreements you may have signed with them are invalid. Safe Security and Mr. Dennis Malcan never had a State license.

Enclosed is an agreement for monitoring only. We have monitored your accounts for free up until now. Our normal monitoring fee is $20.00 per month.

If you wish to continue with our service, please sign the agreement and return it to us.

We will still monitor your account until we hear from you.

Sincerely,

Samuel East
EAST SECURITY

Encls.
SE/cln

Follow these Westroots guidelines for strong sales letters:

○ Attention

○ Desire

○ Persuasion

○ Action.

Here are these elements in more detail.

○ *Attract Your Readers' Attention:* Shock them. Appeal to their self-interest and pride. Hook them. These are techniques Madison Avenue advertisers use successfully to entice us to buy luxury items we believe we have to own. The fact that we've been living without them suddenly disappears. Advertisers notoriously use dramatic attention-getting ads. You might open with a question. Remember, sales promotion letters can overwhelm and get thrown out as soon as they're opened. Your sales letter must attract, yet be pertinent to your audience. State the advantages of your products and services. Look at the excerpt below. This letters appears to have all the elements of an effective sales letter, yet it doesn't overwhelm the reader.

What does Laguna San Rafael Resort and Spa offer the investor?

Laguna San Rafael offers the investor the opportunity to be part of this exciting resort. You only invest in the ownership of your suite, but you can enjoy all the benefits of a premiere destination resort.

You need to know your audience; what seems like an advantage to you might appear as a disadvantage to them. For example, you wouldn't want to try to sell a sports car to an audience consisting of large families unless you specify it could be a good "second" or "fun" car.

○ *Create Desire:* Make your readers want what you have to sell. Show them how their life will improve if they buy your product or service. Remember that the advantages must outweigh the costs. Look at this excerpt. The writer knows the audience consists of beach-property owners, and is appealing to the readers' values as owners of real estate.

> As an owner of a Newport Beach apartment house, you can appreciate the area and the value. I'm proud to currently have exclusively listed one of the finest buildings in Newport Beach.
>
> The property's superior location is on Beach Street, within four blocks of the beach. Only pride of ownership can describe this building. Built fourteen years ago, this one-owner property has had meticulous care inside and out.

○ *Use Persuasion:* This is the "sell." Use facts, statistics, logic, or expert testimony. If you use "expert" testimony, make sure your experts are knowledgeable about your product and not just famous people. Many television commercials ignore this principle and are able to get away with ignoring it because of the fame of their experts—for example, using famous Hollywood stars to sell soft drinks. You probably won't pay millions of dollars for your experts, so use real experts to "tell your truth." But, make the truth believable. If it's not, you'll lose your potential customers.

Have you ever received one of those envelopes that promise millions of dollars if you only fill out the coupon and send it in? They guarantee you're a winner! Do you believe them? If you're like most extremely busy executives, chances are you dump these envelopes in your trash without even opening them. Do you worry that you've thrown away a million dollars? Of course not. These claims are so outrageous that you don't believe them. As a matter of fact, you even get irritated that the sender has thought you're foolish to believe such mockery! Truth is persuasive; exaggeration is not.

○ *Specify the Action To Be Taken:* Tell your readers what you want them to do, how to do it, and when to do it. Be as specific as possible. Don't say, "Please call at your earliest convenience." Instead, say, "Please call 555-5000 by July 1."

Here are three more excerpts from sales letters. See if you can determine which ones work and which ones don't. What are the positive qualities of the effective sales letters? What are the negative qualities of the ineffective ones?

The first one is directed toward business executives who might subscribe to this magazine:

> We would like to take this opportunity to announce a new magazine especially for business executives. You will find many interesting sections that are particularly geared to the problems and concerns of business people across the continent. Our readership includes all types of businesses. . . .

The second one is directed toward a potential real estate investor:

> Would you please take a minute to look at this investment opportunity in Fallbrook? The owners of this property had planned to develop the sites, but the partnership recently decided to sell instead.
>
> The land/value price is underpriced considerably. We think this area will be another Mission Valley in the next couple of years.

This excerpt is directed toward potential luxury car owners:

> We have an exciting job ahead. It's our privilege to introduce a new Italian touring sedan to American drivers. Its name is Panther. It's sleek, fast, and it projects a boldness seldom seen within the staid European automotive establishment. We'll tell you right up front, the Panther combines its driver-oriented technology with a level of comfort designed to be unmatched by other vehicles in its class.

The first example is dry and boring. It loses its reader in the first sentence. The second two excerpts combine much of the elements discussed above. They are effective openings and contain all the elements to keep readers' interest.

COMPLAINT LETTERS

Have you ever accepted poor quality or service in a product you purchased simply because you didn't take the time to write a letter of complaint? If so, you're in the majority. Writing this type of letter doesn't have to be drudgery. You can make it short, to the point, and obtain results. Assertive business practice dictates that you must often write this type of letter.

The first Westroots rule of complaint letter writing: **Never** angrily complain in a complaint letter. If you are hostile and rude, what kind of results do you think you will get? If you answered "None," you're right! Most people, when confronted in this manner, get defensive and angry. Consider this example:

> Dear Sir:
>
> I'm very disappointed in the computer I bought from you last month. The hard disk crashes every time I use it. I called your service representative three times before he returned my calls. He finally came out on a service call but said he could find nothing wrong with it and that it was probably "user error"! Nevertheless, when I started using it again, it crashed once more!
>
> I am hoping that I can obtain some satisfaction after all the inconvenience I have been caused. I expect to hear from you shortly.
>
> Yours truly,
>
>
> John Thomas

Obviously, John Thomas wrote this letter in anger and frustration. Although he doesn't threaten, he also doesn't say what he wants. It's important to tell the reader what you want. Westroots second rule: ask for what you want. Here's a rewrite of Mr. Thomas' complaint letter. Notice the tone. The letter is also more factual and to the point. The writer states what action he expects from the computer dealer:

> Dear Regional Manager:
>
> On June 28, 1987, I purchased an ABC Computer, Model D, with a 40 Megabyte hard disk from your Phoenix store. I purchased the ABC because of its excellent record, and I bought it from Computerville

because of your reputation for service and customer concern.

Unfortunately, I have had a serious problem that has caused me considerable inconvenience and frustration. Following is a sequence of dates and contacts that describe the problem and actions taken to resolve it:

○ June 30, 1987—I called your store and requested service. (I have purchased the service agreement.)

○ July 2—The service representative came and picked up the drive for repair. He checked the drive and fixed it.

○ July 15—The drive malfunctioned again. I lost half my data. I called the service representative. He came and picked up the drive and took it into the shop for repair. Now I was without the use of my computer.

○ July 27—The service representative returned my drive. It worked well for three days.

○ July 30—The same problem recurred that happened on July 15. Note that this is almost a month since I've purchased the computer.

In view of my inconvenience, I am asking that you replace this hard drive as soon as possible. As I urgently need the use of this computer for my business, I would also appreciate a loaner until my machine is in working condition.

Sincerely,

John Thomas

In complaint letters, your tone is crucial. Never sound angry, hostile, vindictive, or threatening when you write your letter. When you write a complaint letter, let it sit for twenty-four hours before you mail it—better yet, have a colleague read it.

Avoid terms such as *complaint, rotten, lemon, disgusted, dishonest, false, untrue,* or other words with negative connotations. Be positive. Here are some specific guidelines for writing complaint letters:

○ Start with an explanation of the problem. Be specific and use dates, amounts, model numbers, and any other concrete information when possible and where appropriate. Use a positive tone and be complimentary about something, if possible.

○ State your inconvenience or loss as succinctly as possible. Again use dates, amounts, and other documentation. Stick to the facts and avoid emotions.

○ State the results or action you expect. This principle is the same as in any business letter. Let your reader know what you want. Avoid threats, such as a loss of business, especially if this is your first communication regarding the problem. You can always threaten later if you must. However, you should reserve this type of communication for your final action.

○ Close in a friendly manner. Indicate your trust in the company so that it can help. Appeal to the company's desire to retain you as a customer and to maintain its reputation for strong customer service.

When you follow these guidelines, you are emphasizing the facts of the situation rather than your emotions. You appeal to your reader's business sense; it's good business to have happy customers. Also, you let the reader determine the specific adjustment appropriate for your situation. It may be enough to state that you will leave the terms of the adjustment up to your reader, but that you do expect some satisfaction or compensation.

One way to answer the complaint letter is through the Adjustment Letter.

ADJUSTMENT LETTERS

What if you receive a complaint letter? The first Westroots rule is to answer it promptly, no matter how inconsequential or offensive it seems to you. If your customer spent the time writing, the letter deserves your response. Your answer should be polite, fair, and logical. Avoid getting defensive or angry, no matter what the tone of the complaint letter.

Here are some Westroots Rules of Adjustment Letters to remember:

○ Begin positively. State the good news immediately if there is any. If not, make some positive statement, such as, "It pleases us that you decided to purchase your first computer from Computerville."

○ Offer a factual explanation of the events leading to the problem. Be specific, concise, and direct. Never overdefend yourself, yet don't blame the customer.

Look at this cold and hostile adjustment letter:

Dear Mr. Thomas:

We are sorry that we cannot satisfy your request. Unfortunately, our company's policy has always been one of "let the buyer beware." That's why we can keep our prices low.

We do offer a ten day return policy. However, since
you have exceeded the time limit, there is really
nothing I can do.

Sincerely,

George C. West
General Manager

Since Mr. Thomas' request was so vague, no wonder Mr.
Hall couldn't satisfy it. Now look at the friendly rewrite of
the same letter that follows. Which do you prefer?

Dear Mr. Thomas:

We are sorry for your trouble and inconvenience.
Unfortunately, there has been a bad shipment of
hard drives installed in some of the ABC Model D's.
You're quite right in expecting better service from
our store.

Since Computerville bases its reputation on customer
service, we will be glad to replace your hard disk as
soon as possible. Unfortunately, we don't have any
Model D's available for a "loaner," but we do have
Model C's and Model B's. If they can't do the job,
perhaps we can provide you with Computerville's
own brand which is comparable to the Model D.

We value you as a Computerville customer. We want
to make every transaction satisfactory to you, and we
hope to resolve this situation.

Sincerely,

George C. West
General Manager

○ *The Customer Is Always Right:* Remember, the
  business edict of "the customer is always
  right." Tell your customer the adjustment
  you are willing to make. If it's not what the
  customer requested, explain why in factual

terms. Apologize, and at the same time, emphasize the positive aspects of your adjustment.

○ *Close with Good Will:* Resell your good name, product, service, and company. Explain that you value your customers and that their business is important to you.

REFINE IT

You aren't finished until you use Westroot Rules of Refining and Proofing discussed in the SPEAKWRITE chapter. Here are some additional techniques for refining your letters before they leave your desk:

○ Keep in mind Westroots basic principle of good writing. Write the way you speak — conversationally and naturally.

○ Avoid needless words and unnecessary jargon.

○ Write with short sentences and paragraphs.

○ Use lists and headings.

○ Use strong action verbs. Avoid "to be" verbs. Use the action verb lists.

○ Simple is strongest. Where possible, substitute short, everyday language.

○ Use smooth transitions between paragraphs. Review the transition word list.

○ Use the active voice. Read more about the active and passive voices in Part 1.

○ If you must use the passive voice, use it consciously and selectively. Use it when you purposely wish to be vague.

○ Ask yourself these questions:

   ○ Have I addressed my intended audience?

   ○ Is my tone friendly and positive?

   ○ Is my purpose clearly stated?

   ○ Do I tell my reader what I want done?

○ Finally, proof your letter one last time using Westroots Proofing Techniques discussed in the SPEAKWRITE chapter.

Now you have the skills to write a perfect letter. Let's move on to Part III.

PART THREE

HELPING YOURSELF TO THE TOOLS OF THE TRADE

CHAPTER 10

Word Processors: Allies or Enemies?

You've been extremely busy. The telephone has interrupted you all day. Desperately you try to finish your draft of the quarterly report on your word processor so you can give it to your assistant for clean up and final editing. Your presentation to the Board of Directors is on Monday morning. The phone rings again. While talking on the phone, you finally decide to save your document since you haven't saved it in three hours. You finish the call, retrieve your document, and a blank screen appears. You panic. What happened? Three hours of work destroyed. The backup has only the latest version from yesterday. You put your head in your hands, realizing you have to work yet another weekend.

If you've been working with word processors, this scenario sounds familiar. You may have considered forgetting about computers altogether! At least your paper and pencil notes won't disappear into the stratosphere!

Unfortunately, anyone who uses computers and word processing programs has probably experienced this type of situation. Many times you probably wonder if this "new" technology really saves time. It does, though.

To those readers who use word processors and want to learn how to maximize their writing and efficiency, this chapter is for you. If you are new to word processing, or are thinking of buying a computer and word processing software, our next chapter refers you to some resources. But the best way to learn about word processing software and computers is to shop around and try them for yourself. Don't be put off by overly technical salespeople. Ask questions and continue shopping.

BENEFITS

Anyone who uses a computer with word processing software knows the final product appears clean, error-free, and professional. In addition, laser printers give documents a typeset, professional appearance.

Word processors also allow you to correct your documents without rewriting or retyping the entire document. In fact, you can go into the document, make several changes quickly, and then print out a perfect copy. You can even create templates of letter and memo formats, copy them into your files, and write your memos and letters on them.

Microcomputers have changed our world. Word processors have changed our business standards. No longer is the typewritten letter with visible white-out or typos acceptable. In fact, if the type style isn't easy to read and professional looking, readers may discount the content of the document. Of course, there are disadvantages, too. We may be so impressed by the physical appearance of documents, that we fail to see if the content is as impressive.

Then there is the technology itself. Some people have gotten so caught up with the technology that they waste time experimenting with the machine when they should be doing their job.

No one can doubt the future of the computer. At first, office personnel feared the replacement of their jobs. But that fear has dissipated. Computers have created more jobs. An entire industry has evolved around them. We need technicians, operators, programmers, technical writers, trainers, maintenance and service people, and often corporate divisions to update and monitor them.

But do they save time? In some areas they do. Picture your assistant struggling to complete a report on the typewriter. He finally finishes the ten-page report, and you discover you omitted an important paragraph on page five. Chances are, he's going to have to retype at least the last five pages. If he were using a word processor, all he would have to do is insert the paragraph and print out the last five pages. What if you're adding charts and graphs? On some computers, you can create those charts and graphs, insert them right into the document, and then print it out.

These are some of the advantages of word processors:

○ Easily change document organization and structure

○ Significantly reduce spelling and typos

○ Completely standardize formats

○ Easily create professional-looking documents

○ Quickly search for commonly misspelled words and phrases containing usage errors.

Here are some drawbacks to keep in mind:

○ Word processing doesn't cut production time in half. Don't throw out your typewriter. You may need it for quickie memos and envelopes. Printing envelopes on your printer is tricky business and not necessarily a time-saver unless you're doing a mass mailing. In that case, you might use the label-making feature in your word processing program and set your printer to print labels. The learning time for word processing programs, although variable, may affect project deadlines. Allow a couple of weeks for everyone to get comfortable with the new system. Don't select a word processor or change word processing software in the middle of a project with tight deadlines.

○ There are some health problems associated with computers, including eyestrain, headaches, backaches, and fatigue.

Studies substantiate that there are health issues to consider when using computers and word processors.

Monitors come in all colors, sizes, shapes, and clarity. The most important considerations are contrast, glare, and clarity of characters. Inexpensive monitors are sometimes blurry and a major contributor to eyestrain. You may need to use a polarizing screen to cut down on glare or to work in a darkened area. Make sure you have proper lighting and a monitor with which you can adjust the contrast. The characters should be clear, easy to read, and sharp.

Make sure you can maintain a comfortable posture since most back problems occur as a result of poor sitting posture. You should have a comfortable chair with back support. Make sure that the keyboard and the monitor are comfortable, the screen is easily readable, the keyboard is functional, and the chair supports your back. Even if you have a comfortable chair with good back support, you may experience back problems. If so, you probably need periodically to get up, walk around and stretch. Isometrics or other exercise can relieve many of your back problems. It may also give you a needed break from your writing, especially if you experience writer's block. Getting some distance from your computer and your writing can help clear up all sorts of problems. Allow yourself and your employees frequent breaks. The breaks don't have to be long.

WRITING WITH A WORD PROCESSOR

Using the SPEAKWRITE system and your word processor, you can easily produce perfect documents. However, just because you are using a computer, don't expect perfect documents on your first attempt.

A computer is an excellent writing tool. As with a good pen, it won't by itself improve your writing, although it may help to make it more legible. Following are some approaches to writing with word processors that we have found useful with SPEAKWRITE.

WESTROOTS RULES OF WRITING WITH A WORD PROCESSOR

○ Do your SPEAK IT work with pen and paper. You can carry them anywhere and jot down ideas for your documents. List the audience, purpose, tone, and results. Use short phrases and sentences.

○ Brainstorm and organize on paper. Mindmap or pyramid here too. Although some people find they like to do all their writing on the computer, we feel it's helpful to do some of your "front-end" work on paper. You don't have to create new files, copy, and move sections around. Doing this can get cumbersome. You may find the technology interfering with your writing.

○ Freewrite with your word processor. Don't stop to correct typos or spelling errors. Refrain from reorganizing sentences and phrases. You will lose your train of thought and interrupt your creative flow.

○ Spell check your freewriting. We suggest this because we know the perfectionists will start to correct spelling immediately. Let the technology work for you.

○ Print out your freewriting. Read it through without making any changes. Then do some pencil editing and reorganizing. Don't feel bound by your edits. When you go back into your document, you may make different changes.

○ Let your document sit for as long as you can afford, preferably a day, at the least a few hours.

○ Revise your document with your word processor. This is the stage when you can pass it off to your assistant depending on how finished you feel your pencil changes are.

Some writers prefer to revise a second time themselves. Then they give the documents to their assistants for final formatting and general cleaning up. Make your heavy changes on this draft. Move around, experimenting with your document.

○ Always do a final spell check, especially after massive changes.

○ Print out another draft and proof carefully. Apply all the Westroots proofing techniques here, since it's very easy to create new errors with the computer.

○ Make final changes and print out a perfectly clean document.

Some of these steps you may be able to skip, especially if the document is short. A word of warning: always proof your documents completely at least twice, no matter how short. Proof them online and then print them out and proof them again. Don't rely on spelling checkers to find all your typos. Especially check words such as *of*, *off*, *on*, *a*. You may have spelled these words correctly, but you may have made an incorrect choice.

CAUTIONS ABOUT WRITING WITH A WORD PROCESSOR

Having the ability to freewrite directly into a word processor sometimes leads to wordiness and lengthy sentences. You can type your thoughts fast.

There's another problem with the technology itself. The technology changes almost every day. It's nearly impossible to keep up with the constantly changing and growing computer industry. Computer books are out-dated by the time they arrive on bookstore shelves. As a matter of fact, this chapter may already be outdated by the time you read it. It was probably outdated by the time it went to print. To keep upgrading your equipment is costly in terms of money and time. Every time you buy a new computer and change software, including upgrading your present programs, there are time costs—including the time it takes for the management functions of upgrading your disks and distributing them to all users, and the time it takes to learn the new software. You may find you need to hire an assistant to handle these additional burdens.

Another problem is with the perfectionist in you. Perfectionism occurs when writers write and rewrite. First of all, don't try to write perfectly the first time. This principle is true whether you're writing with or without a computer. Don't let the freedom the computer allows distract you. Be cautious of making changes. Often, you'll need to reprint an entire document. All this changing and printing takes time. Yes, it takes less time than it would to retype the entire document, but it still takes time. Eventually you must decide on a finishing point. Promise yourself and your staff that you won't keep making inconsequential style changes. Remember, there are many ways to say the same thing. Sometimes your way may be better, but not crucial.

Try not to let the technology take your mind off your work. Sometimes people find themselves immersed in learning all they can about computers, with the result that they are not doing their jobs.

Other problems include the following:

○ Not being able to see your documents in their entirety. With most programs, you can read only twenty-four lines at a time. This may add to your own disorganization and disrupt the continuity of your writing.

○ Easily overlooked typos, usage errors, and grammar errors.

○ The possibility of losing hours of work because of an unforeseen power surge or power outage.

○ Loss of time due to system maintenance and repair.

○ Loss of time due to mechanical malfunctions. This problem is particularly true with printers.

○ High expectations that the finished product always looks good. Sometimes the package looks good, but there's no content.

○ Likelihood of repeating yourself, especially if you reorganize and copy one section to another instead of "moving" one section to another.

MAKING THE COMPUTER YOUR FRIEND

Here are some strategies to help you turn the computer into a powerful tool that enhances your company and your writing.

○ Run frequent spell checks, and then proof again.

○ Make sure you have provisions for someone to service your computer, either a service agreement or an employee who has computer expertise. You don't want to have system breakdowns when you're rushing to meet difficult deadlines.

○ During revision, print often so you can see your document as a whole.

○ Don't overrevise. Because it's so easy to move, delete, and change, be careful not to overly critique your style. Revise grammar.

○ Do your planning with paper and pencil.

○ Freewrite and hand revise. Let your assistants enter revisions and format the final copy.

○ Don't overrely on spelling and style checkers. Never skip proofreading just because you have checked your documents with one or both of these tools.

○ Don't update your software when you're in a time crunch. Keep aware of the technology and how it's being used in your company. Watch for abuses—computer games or employees using the equipment for personal projects.

○ Set up style sheets and templates. Use the technology to its fullest advantage. Don't repeat. Create an index of formats.

○ Back up your work. Many word processors have an automatic backup feature. Use it, because it may save you hours of possible lost work and much frustration.

SPELLING CHECKERS AND THESAURUSES

Your new software probably has at least a 100,000 word dictionary and an 80,000 word thesaurus. Don't be tricked into believing these "miracle cures" will solve all your writing problems.

Spelling checkers are handy tools that are especially useful in finding those overlooked typos you may have missed. They're attractive when they provide a list of possible spellings from which to choose. However, since they can't tell the difference between words like *there* and *they're* and *bare* and *bear*, they do have their limitations. They also can't recognize usage or grammar errors, such as "He are going to the convention."

Spell check your documents every time you print revised documents. But proof them carefully even after you have spell checked them. Even though most word processors allow you to create your own dictionary of words that are not in the program's dictionary, spell check dictionaries don't replace a careful proofreading.

Thesauruses are another story. Many experts contend they have been inserted in word processing software as a marketing device. We caution you not to rely on them, whether they are in book form or a feature of your word processing software.

ELECTRONIC MAIL

Main frame computers usually have an electronic mail system. These days, many companies that have main frame computers encourage their employees to use electronic mail—instead of writing memos and using the telephone. Employees tend to write and communicate more frequently with each other.

When you use your mail, you no longer have to play telephone tag. With electronic mail, you write your colleague the message and send it to her. With some systems, you can tell if the recipient has read the mail. With tele-phone tag, you never know when someone has received a message—or when you'll receive a response.

Electronic mail (e-mail) allows great communication between company branches. You can send a message to your East Coast office in a matter of minutes. No longer is there a need for a run to the express-mail drop box at five o'clock. You can also send documents, not just messages. In addition, you don't need a duplicating machine. E-mail allows you to send several copies of the same correspon-dence to anyone who's on the system. Carbon copies are now "electronic copies."

Although e-mail sounds like a perfect system, it has some problems. E-mail can be too much fun. Employees can get wrapped up in reading messages that don't pertain to them, resulting in a loss of valuable time. Sometimes e-mail becomes a means to spread rumors and complaints. The result can be that busy employees may waste time reading these petty messages, or avoid reading their mail altogether. E-mail works only if there are some guidelines attached to it. Here are some guidelines to make your e-mail system efficient:

○ Use SPEAKWRITE. Writing an electronic mail message is the same as writing a com-pany memo. Remember, you are signing your name to a document that people may save for future reference. Express your thoughts clearly and simply. Use as few words as possible. Remember your action verbs and don't forget tone. Just because e-mail is electronic rather than paper, you shouldn't forget your SPEAKWRITE techniques. They still apply.

○ Either read your messages or delete those which aren't important to you. Sort them by importance so you'll remember to act on them. Either save the message permanently, or print it out to file somewhere else. If you don't have time for this, have an assistant do it for you.

○ Stick to the subject of the message, especially when you're responding to messages. If you have another issue to raise, write a new message. Doing this helps everyone in filing, sorting, and reviewing mail. Just as in a memo, never combine too many points in one message.

These are just a few suggestions on how to use your company's mail system effectively. E-mail is only as effective as the people who use it. Its main objective is to encourage efficiency and communication. But if the people don't have these objectives, the system won't work as it's designed.

If you have an e-mail system in your company, remind your employees that their good writing and communication habits are as important when using the electronic mail system as with any other means of communication.

SOME FINAL THOUGHTS ON WORD PROCESSORS

Word processors won't solve your writing problems. On the contrary, they may create problems you didn't have before your computer days. However, if you proceed cautiously, writing with a word processor can be an enjoyable experience. You will be proud of your finished product.

Word processors are powerful writing tools. They can save time, yet they can also cause frustration and waste time. They can make the writing process more fun, but they can also contribute to backaches and headaches. However, they do allow you the freedom to make changes and try new techniques that your typewriter never provided. Every change on your typewriter required retyping. With word processing, you can make changes and revisions on the computer with a few keystrokes. You can mark questionable sentences or paragraphs that are invisible when you print them out, but visible to you on the screen. Your computer can create a table of contents and an index. You can use your spell check to find those misspelled words you might otherwise overlook. These functions can reduce the tedium and allow you to do the thing you do the best—communicate!

CHAPTER 11

Resources

DICTIONARIES

THESAURUSES

STYLE GUIDES

OTHER BOOKS FOR THE
COMPANY LIBRARY

GRAMMAR REFERENCES

BUSINESS WRITER'S REFERENCES

WORD PROCESSING RESOURCES

When improving, you're bound to get stuck. So what should you do? Go to your bookshelf or your company library. If your company doesn't have a library, it's time to start one. Also, don't forget your local library. If you haven't stepped in a library for years, now's a good time to get acquainted. Every writer needs resource and reference books. You need quick answers to grammar and usage questions. Chances are you're too embarrassed to ask anyone a spelling or punctuation question. If you have a few good reference books with adequate indexes, you're all set.

You may think that your word processor will catch all of your errors with its 100,000 word online dictionary. But these dictionaries are not infallible. You should also have a dictionary on your desk. No self-respecting writer works without one. As a matter of fact, there are several musts in the reference book arena.

Here is a brief list of books that Westroots suggests you keep handy. The comments give you a guide for understanding their contents.

DICTIONARIES

Webster's Ninth New Collegiate Dictionary, Springfield, MA: Merriam-Webster, Inc., 1985.

This dictionary is the best desk dictionary of its kind. It is an abridged version of *Webster's Third New International Dictionary, Unabridged* (Merriam-Webster, Inc., 1961, latest addenda © 1981). Merriam-Webster's is the definitive dictionary, and if you can, have an office copy of the unabridged and desk copies of the abridged. The desk dictionary contains a style guide, punctuation guide, and appendices that include biographical and geographical names, and also foreign words and phrases.

Webster's New World Misspeller's Dictionary. New York: Simon and Schuster, 1983.

This dictionary contains 15,000 common misspellings and their correct spellings. You can look up words the way you think they're spelled; the next column contains the corrections.

Webster's New World Speller/Divider. Rev. ed. New York: Simon and Schuster, 1971.

This dictionary contains a handy listing of 33,000 words for quick reference of spelling, accent, and syllable division.

THESAURUSES

We hesitate to recommend thesauruses, because most writers who use them tend to become overly dependent on them. Their writing becomes stilted and unnatural. Also, remember that a thesaurus suggests synonyms. The suggested synonym might not fit in the context of your sentence. Every word has a different meaning. Choosing synonyms simply to keep from repeating yourself might not work. Consider these examples:

> Our most current project is the Wright Project.
> This project is a multi-million dollar project that
> consists of 100 employees.

Now look at the same sentence rewritten, using a thesaurus. The writer used the first two entries that appeared on her online thesaurus.

> Our most current project is the Wright Project.
> This blueprint is a multi-million dollar design that
> consists of 100 employees.

The words "blueprint" and "design" don't work. Although acceptable synonyms, they are unsuitable choices in this context.

Let's rewrite the sentence without the redundancy and the stilted synonyms:

> Our most current project, the Wright Project, is a
> multi-million dollar job that consists of 100
> employees.

Some possibilities might have worked in this example, such as *venture*, *undertaking*, or *enterprise*. But the writer used *job*. In the context she felt it was a better word choice for this particular "project."

If you need to increase your vocabulary, you're better off using a vocabulary builder than a thesaurus. But if you must use a thesaurus, use it with caution. Reread your sentence carefully. Does it say what you want it to mean? Does it sound stuffy and unnatural? Read it out loud. You may find another word that works better for you. You may even wind up rewriting the sentence. Sometimes thesauruses are good to stimulate your mind. They help you to think about what you are trying to say.

Here are our two recommendations:

Roget, Peter Mark. *Rogets International Thesaurus*. 4th ed. New York: Crowell, 1977.

Although it does not have a dictionary format, this is the most authoritative thesaurus. It's sectioned off by concept and provides users with an index. Since the words are concept-related and not perfect "synonyms," use this reference with extreme caution.

Webster's New Dictionary of Synonyms. Rev. ed. Springfield, MA: Merriam-Webster, 1973.

This "thesaurus" is in an easy-to-use dictionary format. Although the "synonyms" are not perfect, this is a better reference for writers in a hurry. Again, we recommend extreme caution when using this guide because no two words are exactly the same.

STYLE GUIDES

Chicago Manual of Style, The. 13th ed. Chicago: University of Chicago Press, 1982.

If you're looking for a style guide to own, this is it. The 13th edition includes even a guide to electronic publishing. America's top publishing houses have adopted it as their style guide. It is widely accepted and an easy-to-use reference book.

Strunk, William, Jr., and E.B. White. *The Elements of Style*. New York: Macmillan Publishing Co., 1959.

Probably the best and briefest statement of the principal requirements for plain English. This book is the "bible" of serious communication. You don't use this book as a one-time reference; you read it continually.

OTHER BOOKS FOR THE COMPANY LIBRARY

Bernstein, Theodore M. *The Careful Writer*. New York: Atheneum, 1973.

A modern guide to English usage by a *New York Times* managing editor who has also taught at the Columbia School of Journalism. This guide is alphabetically arranged for useful reference. It contains more than 2,000 entries.

Follett, Wilson. *Modern American Usage*. New York: Hill and Wang, 1966.

A guide to educated usage and good taste by a college English professor and university press editor.

Jordan, Lewis. *The New York Times Manual of Style and Usage*. New York: Times Books, 1976.

An enlarged edition of guidelines for those who write and edit. Easy-to-use and very complete. This is the authority for *New York Times* reporters and editors.

Miller, Casey, and Date Swift. *The Handbook of Nonsexist Writing*. New York: Lippincott and Crowell, 1980.

A must for every company libary. This handbook discusses all aspects of sexism in our language, beginning with some historical background. Interesting reading with helpful tips on how to avoid sexism in your writing.

Zinsser, William. *On Writing Well: An Informal Guide to Writing Nonfiction*. 3rd ed. New York: Harper & Row, 1985.

Although not directly related to business writers, this book contains a section addressed to business and technical writing and writing with a word processor. The third edition is filled with inspiration and anecdotes. A great source of encouragement to break writer's block.

GRAMMAR REFERENCES

Although we don't push grammar in this book, there are several good grammar books to use for reference. You should have at least one in your library.

Hodges, John C., and Mary E. Whitten. *Harbrace College Handbook*. New York: Harcourt Brace Jovanovich, Publishers, 1984.

One of the most comprehensive and correct guides for the individual writer.

Perrin, Porter, G. *Writer's Guide and Index to English*. 5th ed., Revised by Wilma R. Ebbitt. Glenview, IL: Scott, Foresman, 1972.

An excellent resource for the business writer. This widely used guide includes chapters on sentences, paragraphs, spelling, and punctuation.

Sabin, William A. *The Gregg Reference Manual*. 6th ed. New York: Gregg Division/McGraw-Hill, 1985.

This handy reference will answer all your questions about grammar, usage, and business convention.

Warriner, John E., May Whitten, and Francis Griffith. *English Grammar and Composition*. New York: Harcourt Brace Jovanovich, 1977.

Extensive grammatical explanations and rules of composition. Practice exercises to improve writing are included in this book.

BUSINESS WRITER'S REFERENCES

Reed, Jeanne. *Business English*. New York: Gregg Division/McGraw Hill Book Company, 1978.

This is a basic adult education text-kit by a business education administrator.

Westheimer, Patricia. *The Perfect Memo*. Glenview, Illinois: Scott, Foresman, 1988.

The companion to *The Executive Style Book*, this book focuses on everything you'll ever want to know about memo writing. It explains the SPEAKWRITE system and shows you how to compose professional, powerful memos. An excellent resource to help you perfect your memos.

Williams, Joseph M. *Style: Ten Lessons in Clarity and Grace*. Glenview, IL: Scott, Foresman, 1979.

Written by a Chicago writing consultant, this handy source book deals specifically with sentences. It is especially helpful for business writers who have sentence problems.

WORD PROCESSING RESOURCES

MAGAZINES

Magazines contain probably the best information on computers. We've suggested a few in this section.

ComputerEdge, formerly *The Byte Buyer, San Diego's Microcomputer Magazine*, P.O. Box 83086, San Diego, CA 92138.

This magazine is geared particularly to computer novices. However, it's a wonderful resource for all computer users. It contains feature articles about the "ins" and "outs" of computing, great advertisements for hardware and software bargains, and a helpful reader's forum.

Infoworld, Circulation Dept., 375 Cochituate Road, Box 837, Framingham, MA 01701.

The *Newsweek* of the computer industry, *Infoworld* is a weekly newsmagazine containing all the weekly news about computers and computing. An excellent resource for what's happening in the industry.

PC Magazine, Ziff Davis Publishing Company, P.O. Box 2445, Boulder, CO 80322.

Contains everything you'd ever want to know about PC hardware and software including extensive reviews. It is a highly respected magazine, and its benchmark tests of hardware and software are well-respected in the industry.

BOOKS

We hesitate to recommend books on word processing, since by the time you read this chapter, the books will probably be out-of-date. However, here are two for general reference.

MacWilliams, Peter. *The Word Processing Book*, New York: Ballantine Publisher, 1984.

A good basic introduction to word processing and computers. Although this book doesn't discuss writing techniques, it introduces the reader to word processing functions and available software.

Zinsser, William. *On Writing Well: An Informal Guide to Writing Nonfiction*. 3rd ed. New York: Harper & Row, 1985.

This is the second time we're recommending Zinsser's book. His third edition contains an excellent chapter on writing with a word processor. That chapter alone is worth the cost of the book.

Use these resources freely and often. The best business writers acknowledge that they often look up questions of punctuation and grammar. They also read style books to help refine their writing. It's said that the mark of intelligence is not knowing all the facts but rather knowing where and how to find them. Now that you have the resources, we encourage you to consult them whenever you have questions. In combination with the information and samples in this book, you will feel educated, accomplished, confident, and contemporary in your writing skills.

A P P E N D I X

SIMPLER WORDS AND PHRASES

INSTEAD OF	TRY
accompany	go with
accomplish	carry out, do
accorded	given
accordingly	so
accrue	add, gain
accurate	correct, exact, right
additional	added, more, other
address	discuss
addressees	you
addressees are requested	(omit), please
adjacent to	next to
advantageous	helpful
adversely impact on	hurt, set back
advise	recommend, tell
afford an opportunity	allow, let
aircraft	plane
allocate	divide, give
anticipate	expect
a number of	some
apparent	clear, plain
appreciable	many
appropriate	(omit), proper, right
approximately	about
as a means of	to
ascertain	find out, learn
as prescribed by	in, under
assist, assistance	aid, help
attain	meet
attempt	try
at the present time	at present, now
be advised	(omit)
benefit	help
by means of	by, with
capability	ability, can
close proximity	near

INSTEAD OF	TRY
combat environment	combat
combined	joint
commence	begin
comply with	follow
component	part
comprise	form, include, make up
concerning	about, on
consequently	so
consolidate	combine, join, merge
constitutes	is, forms, makes up
contains	has
convene	meet
currently	now
deem	believe, consider, think
delete	cut, drop
demonstrate	prove, show
depart	leave
designate	appoint, choose, name
desire	want, wish
determine	decide, figure, find
disclose	show
discontinue	drop, stop
disseminate	give, issue, pass, send
due to the fact that	due to, since, because
during the period	during
effect modifications	make changes
elect	choose, pick
eliminate	cut, drop, end
employ	use
encounter	meet
endeavor	try
ensure	make sure
enumerate	count
equipments	equipment
equitable	fair
equivalent	equal

INSTEAD OF	*TRY*
establish	set up, prove, show
evidenced	showed
evident	clear
exhibit	show
expedite	hasten, speed up
expeditious	fast, quick
expend	spend
expertise	ability, skill
expiration	end
facilitate	ease, help
failed to	didn't
feasible	can be done
females	women
finalize	complete, finish
for a period of	for
for example, ____ etc.	for example, such as
forfeit	give up, lose
for the purpose of	for, to
forward	send
frequently	often
function	act, role, work
furnish	give, send
has a requirement for	needs
herein	here
heretofore	until now
herewith	below, here
however	but
identical	same
identify	find, name, show
immediately	at once
impacted	affected, changed
implement	carry out, start
in accordance with	by, following, per, under
in addition	also, besides, too
in an effort to	to
inasmuch as	since

INSTEAD OF	TRY
in a timely manner	on time, promptly
inception	start
indicate	show, write down
indication	sign
inform	tell
initial	first
initiate	start
in lieu of	instead of
in order that	for, so
in order to	to
in regard to	about, concerning, on
inter alia	(omit)
interface with	meet, work with
interpose no objection	don't object
in the amount of	for
in the event that	if
in the near future	shortly, soon
in the process of	(omit)
in view of	since
in view of the above	so
is applicable to	applies to
is authorized to	may
is in consonance with	agrees with, follows
is responsible for	(omit), handles
it appears	seems
it is	(omit)
it is essential	must, need to
it is requested	please, we request, I request
limitations	limits
limited number	few
magnitude	size
maintain	keep, support
majority of	most
maximum	greatest, largest, most
methodology	method

INSTEAD OF	TRY
minimize	decrease, lessen, reduce
minimum	least, smallest
modify	change
monitor	check, watch
necessitate	cause, need
notify	let know, tell
not later than May 10	by May 10, before May 11
not later than 1600	by 1600
notwithstanding	in spite of, still
numerous	many
objective	aim, goal
obligate	bind, compel
observe	see
on a ____ basis	(omit)
operate	run, use, work
optimum	best, greatest, most
option	choice, way
parameters	limits
participate	take part
perform	do
permit	let
pertaining to	about, of, on
point in time	point, time, now, then
portion	part
possess	have, own
preclude	prevent
previously	before
prioritize	rank
prior to	before
proceed	do, go ahead, try
procure	buy
proficiency	skill
provide	give, offer, say
provided that	if
provides guidance for	guides
purchase	buy

INSTEAD OF	*TRY*
pursuant to	by, following, per, under
reflect	say, show
regarding	about, of, on
relative to	about, on
relocate	move
remain	stay
remainder	rest
remuneration	pay, payment
render	give, make
represent	is
request	ask
require	must, need
requirement	need
reside	live
retain	keep
said, some, such	the, this, that
selection	choice
set forth in	in
similar to	like
solicit	ask for, request
state-of-the-art	latest
submit	give, send
subsequent	later, next
subsequently	after, later, then
substantial	large, much
successfully complete	complete, pass
sufficient	enough
take action to	(omit)
task	ask
terminate	end, stop
the month of	(omit)
there are	(omit), exist
therefore	so
therein	there
there is	(omit), exists
thereof	its, their

INSTEAD OF	TRY
the undersigned	I
the use of	(omit)
timely	prompt
time period	(either one)
transmit	send
under the provisions of	under
until such time as	until
validate	confirm
viable	practical
vice	instead of, versus
warrant	call for, permit
whereas	because, since
with reference to	about
with the exception of	except for
witnessed	saw
your office	you

TRANSITIONS/CONNECTIVES

Link sentences by using such transitional expressions as the following:

ADDITION   moreover, further, furthermore, besides, and, and then, likewise, also, nor, too, again, in addition, equally important, next, first, secondly, thirdly, etc., finally, last, lastly

CONTRAST   but, yet, and yet, however, still, nevertheless, on the contrary, after all, for all that, in contrast to this, at the same time, although this may be true, otherwise

COMPARISON   similarly, likewise, in like manner

PURPOSE   to this end, for this purpose, with this object

RESULT   hence, therefore, accordingly, consequently, thus, as a result

TIME   meanwhile, at length, immediately, soon, after a few days, in the meantime, afterward, later, now, then

PLACE   here, there, beyond, nearby, far, opposite to, adjacent to, on the opposite side

SUMMARY, REPETITION, EXEMPLIFICATION, INTENSIFICATION   to sum up, in brief, on the whole, in sum, in short, as I have said, in other words, to be sure, for example, for instance, in fact, indeed

Use short spoken transitions over long, bookish ones. Save long transitions for variety. By using short ones, you help set an ordinary tone for the rest of what you say.

MORE FORMAL	MORE RELAXED
consequently	so
however	but
in addition	also
nevertheless	still

REDUNDANT REDUNDANCIES

at this point
in time
basic essentials
black in color
close proximity
consensus of
opinion
continue on
end result
final conclusion

may possibly
mutual
cooperation
necessary
requisite
one a.m. in
the morning
original
founder
part and parcel

plan in advance
quite unique
reason why
refer back to
resume again
right and
proper
round in shape
safe and sound
two equal
halves

POMPOUS WORDS AND WINDY PHRASES

INSTEAD OF	USE
afford an opportunity	allow
an example of this is the fact that	for example
call your attention to the fact that	remind you
due to the fact that	because
exhibit a tendency to	tend to
for the purpose of	for, to
in reference to	about, regarding
in the majority of circumstances	usually
in the normal course of our procedure	normally
in view of the fact that	because
it is interesting to note that	(delete)

LITTLE QUALIFIERS

a great many	just	pretty
a number of	little	quite
as far as we know	more or less	reasonably
considerably	nearly	seems
essentially	on the whole	to some degree
generally	possibly	very

JARGON...

...conceals a simple idea in a thick fog of words, using circumlocutions instead of going straight to the point, preferring abstract nouns to concrete ones, concentrating on sound rather than sense.

conceptualize	overview	prioritize
facilitate	paradigm	proactive
impact (verb)	parameter	quantify

PREPOSITIONS

The overuse of prepositional phrases can lengthen your sentences and obscure your meaning. Here's a list of prepositions to alert you to prepositional phrases.

about	concerning	out
above	despite	outside
across	down	over
after	during	
against		since
along	except	through
among	for	throughout
around	from	till
at		to
	in	toward
before	inside	
behind	into	under
below		underneath
beneath	like	until
beside		up
besides	near	upon
between	of	
beyond	off	with
by	on	within
	onto	without

WEAK VERBS

Here's a list of the "to be" verbs and other weak verbs to avoid. Use action verbs instead. Suggested action verbs follow on the next pages.

am	has
appear	have
are	is
be	make
became	might
become	seem
been	shall
being	should
could	was
did	were
do	will
had	would

ACTION VERBS

act
activate
adapt
address
adopt
advertise
advise
analyze
anticipate
apply
appraise
arrange
assemble
assess
assist
attain
audit

budget
build

calculate
catalogue
change
chart
classify
coach
collect
communicate
compile
complete
compose
compute
conduct
confront
conserve
consolidate
construct

consult
contract
control
coordinate
correspond
counsel
create

defer
define
delegate
deliver
demonstrate
design
detail
detect
determine
develop
devise
diagnose
direct
discover
dispense
display
disprove
dissect
distribute
divert
draft
dramatize

edit
educate
electrify
eliminate
enforce
enlarge

entertain
estimate
evaluate
examine
exhibit
expand
explain
express
extract

familiarize
file
filter
figure
fix
formulate
forward

gather
govern
guide

head
help
hire

identify
illustrate
improve
index
indoctrinate
influence
inform
initiate
innovate
inspect
inspire
install
institute

instruct
integrate
interpret
interview
introduce
invent
inventory
investigate

judge

lead
lecture

maintain
manage
map
market
measure
mediate
model
modify
monitor
motivate

navigate
negotiate

observe
obtain
operate
order
organize
originate

paint
participate
perfect
perform
persuade
photograph
pilot

pioneer
plan
play
predict
prepare
prescribe
preserve
preside
print
process
produce
program
project
promote
propose
protect
provide
publicize
purchase

quote

raise
reason
recommend
reconcile
record
recruit
reduce
refer
rehabilitate
render
reorganize
repair
replace
report
represent
research
resolve
respond

restore
retrieve
review
revise
rewrite

save
schedule
select
shape
simplify
sketch
solve
sort
spark
specify
stimulate
straighten
streamline
strengthen
study
suggest
summarize
supervise
supply
survey
synthesize
systematize

tabulate
talk
test
time
train
transcribe
transfer
translate
transmit
treat
tutor

unify   vitalize
upgrade
update   write

FREQUENTLY MISSPELLED WORDS

Here is a list of spelling demons. Keep these handy as a quick reference for those hard-to-spell words.

abbreviate	affidavit	appearance
absence	aggressive	applicable
acceptable	aging	applicant
accessible	agreeable	appointment
accidentally	aisle	appraisal
accommodate	alcohol	appreciable
accompanying	alleged	appropriate
accomplish	allotment	approximate
accordance	allotted	arbitrary
accumulate	allowable	architect
accuracy	allowance	arguing
achievement	all right	argument
acknowledg-ment	already	arrangement
acquaintance	altogether	article
acquire	amateur	ascertain
acquisition	ambitious	assessment
across	amendment	assignment
address	amortization	assistance
adjacent	amortize	associate
adjourn	analysis	assured
adjustment	analyze	athlete
advantageous	announce	athletics
advice	announcement	attendance
advisable	annual	attendant
advise	answer	attorneys
advised	apologize	authentic
adviser	appall	authorize
advisory	apparatus	autumn
	apparent	auxiliary

available
average
awkward

bachelor
bankruptcy
bargain
basis
believable
believe
beneficial
beneficiary
benefited
biased
biennially
bookkeeper
brilliant
brochure
budget
bulletin
bureau
bureaucracy
business

calendar
campaign
canceled
cancellation
candidate
candor
casualty
catalogue
cease
ceiling
challenge
changeable
characteristic
chief
choice
choose

chronological
circumstances
cliche
client
clientele
climatic
coincidence
collateral
column
commission
commitment
committee
comparable
compelled
competent
competition
competitor
compromise
concede
conceivable
conceive
concession
concurred
condemn
conference
confidant
confident
confidential
confidentially
congratulate
connoisseur
conscience
conscientious
conscious
consensus
consequence
consignment
consistent
conspicuous

consular
continual
continuous
controlling
controversy
convenience
convenient
cordially
correlate
correspon-
    dence
correspondents
council
counsel
counselor
counterfeit
courteous
courtesy
creditor
criticism
criticize
current
customer

debtor
deceased
deceive
decision
deductible
defendant
defense
deferred
deficit
definite
definitely
delegate
dependent
depositors
describe

desert
desirable
desolate
deteriorate
develop
development
device
devise
differed
difference
director
disappear
disappoint
discrepancy
dissatisfied
division
dual

eagerly
economical
effect
efficiency
efficient
either
eligible
eliminate
eminent
emphasis
emphasize
employee
endeavor
endorsement
enterprise
enthusiasm
envelop
envelope
environment
equipment
equipped

equivalent
especially
essential
etiquette
evident
exaggerate
exceed
excellence
excellent
except
excessive
exclusively
exercise
existence
expedite
expenditure
experience
explanation
extension
extraordinary

facilities
familiarize
fascinate
favorable
favorite
feasible
February
financial
forcible
foreign
foreword
forfeit
formerly
forward
fourth
freight
friend
fulfillment

furthermore

gauge
genuine
governor
grateful
grievance
guarantee

handled
harass
hardware
hazardous
height
hesitant
hindrance

identical
illegible
immediately
imminent
impasse
imperative
implement
inasmuch as
incidentally
inconvenience
incurred
independent
indispensable
individual
inducement
inference
inferred
influential
innocuous
inquiry
installment
intelligence
intention

intercede
intercession
interfere
interrupted
inventory
investor
irregular
irrelevant
itemized
itinerary
its
it's

jeopardize
judgment
justifiable

knowledge

laboratory
legible
legitimate
leisure
letterhead
liaison
library
license
likable
likelihood
livelihood
loose
lose
luncheon

magazine
maintenance
management
manufacturer
manuscript
maximum
memorandum

merchandise
mileage
minimum
minuscule
miscellaneous
mischievous
modernize
mortgage

necessary
negligible
negotiate
neighborhood
neither
nevertheless
ninety
noticeable

oblige
occasion
occupant
occurred
occurrence
occurring
offense
offering
official
omission
oneself
opportunity
optional
ordinary
organization
organize
original
overdue

pamphlet
parallel
partial

participant
particularly
perceive
percent
performance
permanent
permissible
permitted
perseverance
personal
personnel
persuade
planning
pleasant
pleasure
practical
practically
practice
precede
precision
preferable
preference
preferred
prejudice
preliminary
premium
principal
principle
privilege
procedure
proceed
professor
prominent
prosecute
psychology
purchase
pursue

quantity

questionnaire
quiet
quite

realize
reasonable
receipt
receive
recognize
recommend
recurrence
reference
referred
referring
regrettable
reign
reimburse
remittance
renewal
repetition
representative
requirement
respectfully
respectively
responsible
restaurant
ridiculous
route

salable
satisfactorily
satisfying
schedule
secretary
securities
seized
separate

serviceable
severely
shipment
siege
significant
similar
simultaneous
sincerity
somewhat
specialize
specialty
stationary
stationery
statistics
strength
strictly
submitted
subpoena
subscriber
substantial
succeed
successful
sufficient
superintendent
supersede
supervisor
supposedly
surveillance
survey

tariff
temporary
their
there
thorough
throughout

tragedy
transferred
truism
typing

ultimately
unanimous
undoubtedly
unfortunately
unnecessary
unusually
until
usually

vacillate
vacuum
valuable
vandalize
various
vary
vehicle
vendor
visible
volume
voluntary
volunteer

warehouse
weather
whether
wholly
wield
withhold
worthwhile
writing

yield

EXERCISES

Revise the following sentences using the SPEAKWRITE principles. After you've rewritten these sentences, turn to the suggested revisions.

DECREASE SENTENCE LENGTH.

1. In 1987 then corporate vice-president Stephen Fromm, a dynamic speaker and organizer, established a new company, The Income Organization and he persuaded a number of supervisors and managers to come to work for him.

2. If this method of operation is continued it does raise the issue of why we are marketing a similar product abroad, however, we could discuss it further in Washington, D.C., at our annual meeting.

3. Because of the complexities of the situation I have decided to pay the full assessment on the property and consequently I have directed the Board of Governors to begin proceedings to provide The Seal Company with adequate funds to cover this initial expense.

4. The purpose of the workshop was to discuss state, local, and federal water quality regulations, the economic impact of waste control and concepts and methods of monitoring wastes.

5. Other company departments, including Economics on the seventh floor, are much more flexible than the Library.

6. There are presently three supermarkets supplying Orlando, the Superstore, Pricerite, and Goodbuy.

OMIT NEEDLESS WORDS.

7. Below are provided general guidelines which should be followed for review purposes.

8. There appear to be a number of good quality prospect areas that could be developed in a short period of time.

9. Thank you for your letter of August 5 with respect to work in connection with our new terminal.

10. On April 5, 1984, a trip was made by B. Shore and J. Adams to Baltimore, Maryland for the purpose of attending the MBI Conference on Management Techniques. The scope and subject areas covered by the MBI Conference are described herein.

11. In regard to the upcoming sessions in the training program, it was felt that our employees could substantially benefit from exposure to professional instruction in the areas of technical and business communication.

12. An additional statement will be added to the report.

AVOID STUFFY LANGUAGE.

13. Further to our telephone conversation this morning, I take pleasure in forwarding your requested information.

14. We are in receipt of your letter of February 20, 1987.

15. As per our phone conversation, here is a list of the reports we *must* receive.

16. We are enclosing herewith our check in the amount of $475.64.

17. While preparing for this meeting, Joan and I have identified an issue that may have an impact on the direction of the Education Research project.

18. I would greatly appreciate your help in expediting this request as the current process generates a lot more paperwork on both of our sides.

19. All aspects of the situation should be taken into careful consideration prior to the implementation of any corrective action.

Here are some straightforward pieces of writing. Just for fun, rewrite them and make them as wordy and pompous as you can.

20. It turns out that the director's plan is the most efficient and least expensive way to go.

21. Please call me if you have any other questions.

USE STRONG VERBS.

22. It is our hope that this situation will be improved.

23. All applications being put on research should have initials!

24. An account with a check-guarantee service is a combination of an ABC account and a SuperCard or XYZ credit card.

25. In accordance with your request of March 27, we have developed the attached procedure covering computation of actual freight paid, comparison of actual freight with standard freight, and preparation of shipping schedules.

26. Last week a directive was sent out to all members of this department.

27. The complete schedule cannot be met by Mission Center Corporation.

28. Distribution will be expanded by Computers Incorporated over the next two years.

29. I was informed by Acar that if you had rented the car with free mileage, your total charges would have been $237.45.

30. The policies and procedures for our department are developed by Quality Control.

SUGGESTED REVISIONS

DECREASE SENTENCE LENGTH.

1. In 1987 then corporate vice-president Stephen Fromm, a dynamic speaker and organizer, established a new company, The Income Organization. He persuaded a number of supervisors and managers to come to work for him.

2. If we continue with this method of operation, it will raise the issue of marketing similar products abroad. However, we could discuss it further in Washington, D.C., at our annual meeting.

3. Because of the situation complexities, I have decided to pay the full assessment on the property. Consequently, I have directed the Board of Governors to begin proceedings to cover this initial expense.

4. The workshop discussed:
    - State, local, and federal water quality regulations
    - The economic impact of waste control
    - Concepts and methods of monitoring wastes.

5. The Library is not as flexible as other departments.

6. Three supermarkets supply Orlando: the Superstore, Pricerite, and Goodbuy.

OMIT NEEDLESS WORDS.

7. Follow the guidelines below for review.

8. We could develop several quality prospect areas shortly.
    or
    Quality prospect areas could be developed soon.

9. Thank you for your August 5 letter concerning work in our new terminal.

10. On April 5, 1984, B. Shore and J. Adams attended the MBI Conference on Management Techniques in Baltimore, Maryland. The MBI Conference covered the following subjects:

11. Our employees could benefit substantially from instruction in technical and business communication.

12. We will include an additional statement.

AVOID STUFFY LANGUAGE.

13. I'm sending you the information you requested.

14. We received your February 20 letter.

15. Here is a list of reports we need.

16. Enclosed is our check for $475.64.

17. Joan and I identified an issue that may influence the direction of the Educational Research project.

18. I appreciate your help in speeding up the request. The current process causes excessive paperwork.

19. Consider everything before taking corrective action.

20. The plans of the director, which she gave us, are more efficient than the other plans, and they are also the least expensive expenditures under the circumstances.

21. If you have any comments or questions, do not hesitate to pick up the phone and call me at any time at your earliest possible convenience.

USE STRONG VERBS.

22. We hope the situation improves.

23. Initial all research applications.

24. A check-guarantee service combines an ABC account and a SuperCard or XYZ credit card.

25. Following your March 27 request, we have developed the attached procedure covering:

    o Computation of actual freight paid
    o Comparison of actual freight with standard freight
    o Preparation of shipping schedules.

26. Last week we sent a directive to all department members.

27. Mission Center Corporation cannot meet the complete schedule.

28. Computers Incorporated will expand distribution over the next two years.

29. Acar says if you had rented the car with free mileage, charges would have been $237.45.

30. Quality Control develops our department policies and procedures.

WESTROOTS will evaluate your writing.

Send:

- o Up to one page of your writing
- o $25.00 (covers critique, postage, and handling)
- o Your name and address.

To: WESTROOTS BUSINESS WRITING
SYSTEMS, INC.
3131-A Via Alicante
La Jolla, California 92037

Please allow 4–6 weeks for your critique.

I N D E X

Here's how to receive your free catalog and save money on your next book order from Scott, Foresman and Company:

Simply mail in the response card below to receive your free copy of our latest catalog featuring business and computer books. After you've looked through the catalog and you're ready to place your order, attach the coupon below to receive $1.00 off of catalog price on your next order of Scott, Foresman and Company Publishing Group business or computer books.

✄ —

YES, **please send me my free catalog of your latest business and computer books!**

NAME (please print) _____

COMPANY _____

ADDRESS _____

CITY _____ STATE _____ ZIP _____

Mail response card to:

Scott, Foresman and Company
Professional Publishing Group
1900 East Lake Avenue
Glenview, IL 60025

✄ —

PUBLISHER'S COUPON   NO EXPIRATION DATE

SAVE $1.00

Limit one per order. Good only on Scott, Foresman and Company Professional Publishing Group publications. Consumer pays any sales tax. Coupon may not be assigned, transferred, or reproduced. Coupon will be redeemed by Scott, Foresman and Company, Professional Publishing Group, 1900 East Lake Avenue, Glenview, IL 60025.

Customer's Signature _____